INVADED
BY LOVE

Also by the same author

1500 Illustrations for Preaching and Teaching

INVADED BY LOVE

An Anthology of Christian Conversion Stories

COMPILED BY

ROBERT BACKHOUSE

Marshall Pickering
An Imprint of HarperCollins*Publishers*

Marshall Pickering is an Imprint of
HarperCollins*Religious*
Part of HarperCollins*Publishers*
77–85 Fulham Palace Road, London W6 8JB

First published in Great Britain
in 1993 by Marshall Pickering

1 3 5 7 9 10 8 6 4 2

A catalogue record for this book is
available from the British Library

ISBN 0 551 02327 9

Typeset by Watermark, Crostwight, Norfolk
Printed and bound in Great Britain by
Hartnolls Ltd., Bodmin, Cornwall

To
Roberta and Althea

CONTENTS

9

10

12

15

16

INTRODUCTION

Christian conversion has been defined in numerous ways and, sadly, has sometimes been the subject of heated debate, even among Christians. Part of a verse from the Acts of the Apostles (26:20) provides one helpful definition of conversion: "they should repent and turn to God". Christian conversion has these two elements: turning from sin (repentance), and turning to God for forgiveness (faith). Another helpful definition of conversion is "committing all I know of myself to all I know of Christ". The following conversion stories have been selected on the basis of these definitions.

Experiences of Christ subsequent to conversion are not the subject of this book, but they have not been totally excluded. Thus, for example, the present Archbishop of Canterbury's post-conversion experience has been included.

Well-known as well as unknown people from across the world, over the twenty centuries of Christianity, inspire us as we view the work of God's Spirit invading lives with Christ's love.

Robert Backhouse
Crostwight, Norfolk
Eastertide 1992

Peter preaches at Pentecost

Then Peter stood up with the Eleven, raised his voice and addressed the crowd: "Fellow Jews and all of you who are in Jerusalem, let me explain this to you; listen carefully to what I say. These men are not drunk, as you suppose. It's only nine in the morning! No, this is what was spoken by the prophet Joel:

> 'In the last days, God says,
>   I will pour out my Spirit on all people.
> Your sons and daughters will prophesy,
>   your young men will see visions,
>   your old men will dream dreams.
> Even on my servants, both men and women,
>   I will pour out my Spirit in those days,
>   and they will prophesy.
> I will show wonders in the heaven above
>   and signs on the earth below,
>   blood and fire and billows of smoke.
> The sun will be turned to darkness
>   and the moon to blood
>   before the coming of the great and glorious day of the Lord.
> And everyone who calls
>   on the name of the Lord will be saved.'

"Men of Israel, listen to this: Jesus of Nazareth was a man accredited by God to you by miracles, wonders and signs, which God did among you through him, as you yourselves know. This man was handed over to you by God's set purpose and foreknowledge; and you, with the help of wicked men, put him to death by nailing him to the cross. But God raised him from the dead, freeing him from the agony of death, because it was impossible for death to keep its hold on him. David said about him:

> 'I saw the Lord always before me.
>   Because he is at my right hand,
>   I will not be shaken.
> Therefore my heart is glad and my tongue rejoices;
>   my body also will live in hope,

21

because you will not abandon me to the grave,
  nor will you let your Holy One see decay.
You have made known to me the paths of life;
  you will fill me with joy in your presence.'

"Brothers, I can tell you confidently that the patriarch David died and was buried, and his tomb is here to this day. But he was a prophet and knew that God had promised him on oath that he would place one of his descendants on his throne. Seeing what was ahead, he spoke of the resurrection of the Christ, that he was not abandoned to the grave, nor did his body see decay. God has raised this Jesus to life, and we are all witnesses of the fact. Exalted to the right hand of God, he has received from the Father the promised Holy Spirit and has poured out what you now see and hear. For David did not ascend to heaven, and yet he said,

'The Lord said to my Lord:
  "Sit at my right hand
until I make your enemies
  a footstool for your feet."'

"Therefore let all Israel be assured of this: God has made this Jesus, whom you crucified, both Lord and Christ."

When the people heard this, they were cut to the heart and said to Peter and the other apostles, "Brothers, what shall we do?"

Peter replied, "Repent and be baptised, every one of you, in the name of Jesus Christ so that your sins may be forgiven. And you will receive the gift of the Holy Spirit. The promise is for you and your children and for all who are far off – for all whom the Lord our God will call."

With many other words he warned them; and he pleaded with them, "Save yourselves from this corrupt generation." Those who accepted his message were baptised, and about three thousand were added to their number that day.

Acts 2:14–41

Paul preaches in Antioch in Pisidia

From Paphos, Paul and his companions sailed to Perga in Pamphylia, where John left them to return to Jerusalem. From Perga they went on to Pisidian Antioch. On the Sabbath they entered the synagogue and sat down. After the reading from the Law and the Prophets, the synagogue rulers sent word to them, saying, "Brothers, if you have a message of encouragement for the people, please speak."

Standing up, Paul motioned with his hand and said: "Men of Israel and you Gentiles who worship God, listen to me! The God of the people of Israel chose our fathers; he made the people prosper during their stay in Egypt, with mighty power he led them out of that country, he endured their conduct for about forty years in the desert, he overthrew seven nations in Canaan and gave their land to his people as their inheritance. All this took about 450 years.

"After this, God gave them judges until the time of Samuel the prophet. Then the people asked for a king, and he gave them Saul son of Kish, of the tribe of Benjamin, who ruled for forty years. After removing Saul, he made David their king. He testified concerning him: 'I have found David son of Jesse a man after my own heart; he will do everything I want him to do.'

"From this man's descendants God has brought to Israel the Saviour Jesus, as he promised. Before the coming of Jesus, John preached repentance and baptism to all the people of Israel. As John was completing his work, he said: 'Who do you think I am? I am not that one. No, but he is coming after me, whose sandals I am not worthy to untie.'

"Brothers, children of Abraham, and you God-fearing Gentiles, it is to us that this message of salvation has been sent. The people of Jerusalem and their rulers did not recognise Jesus, yet in condemning him they fulfilled the words of the prophets that are read every Sabbath. Though they found no proper ground for a death sentence, they asked Pilate to have him executed. When they had carried out all that was

23

written about him, they took him down from the tree and laid him in a tomb. But God raised him from the dead, and for many days he was seen by those who had travelled with him from Galilee to Jerusalem. They are now his witnesses to our people.

"We tell you the good news: What God promised our fathers he has fulfilled for us, their children, by raising up Jesus. As it is written in the second Psalm:

> 'You are my son;
>   today I have become your Father.'

The fact that God raised him from the dead, never to decay, is stated in these words:

> 'I will give you the holy and sure blessings promised to David.'

So it is stated elsewhere:

> 'You will not let your Holy One see decay.'

"For when David had served God's purpose in his own generation, he fell asleep; he was buried with his fathers and his body decayed. But the one whom God raised from the dead did not see decay.

"Therefore, my brothers, I want you to know that through Jesus the forgiveness of sins is proclaimed to you. Through him everyone who believes is justified from everything you could not be justified from by the law of Moses. Take care that what the prophets have said does not happen to you:

> 'Look, you scoffers,
>   wonder and perish,
> for I am going to do something in your days
>   that you would never believe,
>   even if someone told you.'"

As Paul and Barnabas were leaving the synagogue, the people invited them to speak further about these things on the next Sabbath. When the congregation was dismissed, many of the Jews and devout converts to Judaism followed Paul and Barnabas, who talked with them and urged them to continue in the grace of God.

On the next Sabbath almost the whole city gathered to hear the word of the Lord. When the Jews saw the crowds, they were filled with jealousy and talked abusively against what Paul was saying.

Then Paul and Barnabas answered them boldly: "We had to speak the word of God to you first. Since you reject it and do not consider yourselves worthy of eternal life, we now turn to the Gentiles. For this is what the Lord has commanded us:

'I have made you a light for the Gentiles,
that you may bring salvation to the ends of the earth.'"

When the Gentiles heard this, they were glad and honoured the word of the Lord; and all who were appointed for eternal life believed.

The word of the Lord spread through the whole region. But the Jews incited the God-fearing women of high standing and the leading men of the city. They stirred up persecution against Paul and Barnabas, and expelled them from their region. So they shook the dust from their feet in protest against them and went to Iconium.

Acts 13:13–51

ACTS (3)   *Explaining the Scriptures*
Paul teaches in the synagogue in Thessalonica

When they had passed through Amphipolis and Apollonia, they came to Thessalonica, where there was a Jewish synagogue. As his custom was, Paul went into the synagogue, and on three Sabbath days he reasoned with them from the Scriptures, explaining and proving that the Christ had to suffer and rise from the dead. "This Jesus I am proclaiming to you is the Christ," he said. Some of the Jews were persuaded and joined Paul and Silas, as did a large number of God-fearing Greeks and not a few prominent women.

Acts 17:1–4

The Bereans receive the Gospel message

As soon as it was night, the brothers sent Paul and Silas away
to Berea. On arriving there, they went to the Jewish
synagogue. Now the Bereans were of more noble character
than the Thessalonians, for they received the message with
great eagerness and examined the Scriptures every day to see
if what Paul said was true. Many of the Jews believed, as did
also a number of prominent Greek women and many Greek
men.

Acts 17:10–12

Paul preaches in the Areopagus at Athens

While Paul was waiting for them in Athens, he was greatly distressed to see that the city was full of idols. So he reasoned in the
synagogues with the Jews and the God-fearing Greeks, as well
as in the market-place day by day with those who happened to
be there. A group of Epicurean and Stoic philosophers began to
dispute with him. Some of them asked, "What is this babbler
trying to say?" Others remarked, "He seems to be advocating
foreign gods." They said this because Paul was preaching the
good news about Jesus and the resurrection.

Then they took him and brought him to a meeting of the
Areopagus, where they said to him, "May we know what this
new teaching is that you are presenting? You are bringing
some strange ideas to our ears, and we want to know what
they mean." (All the Athenians and the foreigners who lived
there spent their time doing nothing but talking about and listening to the latest ideas.)

Paul then stood up in the meeting of the Areopagus and
said: "Men of Athens! I see that in every way you are very
religious. For as I walked around and observed your objects
of worship, I even found an altar with this inscription: TO AN
UNKNOWN GOD. Now what you worship as something

unknown I am going to proclaim to you.

"The God who made the world and everything in it is the Lord of heaven and earth and does not live in temples built by hands. And he is not served by human hands, as if he needed anything, because he himself gives all men life and breath and everything else. From one man he made every nation of men, that they should inhabit the whole earth; and he determined the times set for them and the exact places where they should live. God did this so that men would seek him and perhaps reach out for him and find him, though he is not far from each one of us. 'For in him we live and move and have our being.' As some of your own poets have said, 'We are his offspring.'

"Therefore since we are God's offspring, we should not think that the divine being is like gold or silver or stone—an image made by man's design and skill. In the past God overlooked such ignorance, but now he commands all people everywhere to repent. For he has set a day when he will judge the world with justice by the man he has appointed. He has given proof of this to all men by raising him from the dead."

When they heard about the resurrection of the dead, some of them sneered, but others said, "We want to hear you again on this subject." At that, Paul left the Council. A few men became followers of Paul and believed. Among them was Dionysius, a member of the Areopagus, also a woman named Damaris, and a number of others.

Acts 17:16–34

KRISS AKABUSI   *Come and say "Hi"*
British athlete

Competitors in the 1986 Commonwealth Games in Edinburgh found copies of the Good News New Testament in their hotel rooms, and Kriss Akabusi read the whole of his because he was so spiritually hungry.

From his earliest days he had measured his success by material possessions, acquired through becoming famous, but by 1986 he had begun to realize that no sooner had he acquired one thing than he wanted something bigger and better. He was fascinated by the New Testament and cross-checked its statements in other books. He even saw significance in the fact that the whole calendar, including his own date of birth, took Jesus as its point of reference.

One night in America he prayed, "Lord, if you are there, and I really don't know if you are, you'd better come and say 'Hi' to Kriss." And he became aware of Jesus with him. He is certain that he has been a Christian from that day on, entering into a relationship with God which is real and eternal.

LORD ALEXANDER
British politician
The Word made flesh

From a poor home Alexander went on to be a keen worker for the co-operative movement, a member of Parliament, First Lord of the Admiralty, Minister of Defence and finally Leader of the Opposition in the House of Lords. But his work was built on a commitment to Christ made when he was 20 and attended a Baptist church in Weston-super-Mare. In his testimony to the House of Lords, Alexander said that he had been brought up in the Church of England, and would have stayed there all his life if he had not discovered for himself a truth that was far bigger and wider. This truth was that family and traditional religion are not enough. To gain salvation, he needed to be born again; he needed to go to the Word of God because it is the Word made flesh who gives life.

He learned, and said publicly, that politics would not bring about the kingdom of God.

BROTHER ANDREW
Smuggler of Bibles into Communist lands and founder of Open Doors International
"Let my people go"

Brother Andrew found himself taking an instant dislike to the man who started to address the Christian meeting he was attending. He could hardly restrain his own laughter as the preacher prayed aloud for the eternal welfare of everybody present. Brother Andrew and his friends so disrupted this man's praying that he gave up and quickly asked for the choir to take over. They sang the moving song, "Let my people go".

This seemingly inconsequential event caused Brother Andrew's conversion. The date was 1950. The place was Holland. Brother Andrew lay in bed while a wintry storm raged outside. He imagined that he could hear many noises in the howling wind, but the one that drowned all the rest was the singing of "Let my people go" in that large tent. After a tussle Brother Andrew decided to give up his pride, and he handed himself over to God as he turned over in bed. He says that he may not have exercized a great deal of faith when he prayed, "Lord, if You will show me the way, I will follow You. Amen." However, it was a real and a simple prayer and one that revolutionized his whole life.

C. F. ANDREWS   *Childhood fever*
Missionary in India,
friend and biographer of Mahatma Gandhi

When I was between four and five years old, a very severe attack of rheumatic fever nearly proved fatal. For many months my life was almost despaired of and the suffering was very great ...

My first conscious thoughts about God and Christ were implanted in me at this time by my mother, for I was very close to death, and she used to tell me of the love of Christ for little children and how He took them in his arms and blessed them ...

Outwardly, I was living a strictly religious life, in the bosom of our family, going regularly with my father and mother to church; but inwardly a conflict was going on deep down in the subconscious part of my being, and for a long time this remained unresolved.

Then came a wonderful conversion of my heart to God at the age of nineteen, when I was just about to enter college at Cambridge. So wonderful was it that it changed my whole inner life and released me from the bondage of sin which had bound me fast. Let me tell here very briefly what happened; for it was the great turning-point of my life.

One night the burden of the extreme evil of what I was doing came quite unexpectedly upon me as I knelt down at my bedside to say my prayers. For long hours of darkness I cried out in agony of my spirit. Then, out of my utter need and helplessness, came a marvellous sense of pardon and release. From that moment the new life in Christ began, which was veritably a new birth. His grace and love flooded my whole being.

The days that followed were like a glorious dream. I seemed to be living in a different world of light and love and peace. It illuminated the glory of Nature, and made me love everyone I met.

The effect of this inflow of the Spirit, which came from Christ, was immediately to send me among the poor. Though, up to that time, I was quite unacquainted with that work of service in Christ's name, an inner compulsion seemed to drive me towards it; and all through my life the impulse to surrender all for Christ's sake and to find Him among those who are in need has been present with me so strongly that sooner or later everything has had to give way before it.

"A Pilgrim's Progress", C. F. Andrews, in *Religion in Transition*, Allen & Unwin, 1937, pp. 60–65

METROPOLITAN ANTHONY OF SOUROZH
Christ's presence

Atheist who became a Russian Orthodox priest

Anthony decided that he would not listen to the speaker because he was a priest. But he found that he did listen and that he was indignant about what he heard about Jesus Christ and Christianity. When he arrived home Anthony took a book of the four Gospels off the bookshelf and decided that he would see if what the priest had said was true. Because he wanted to get this over and done with as quickly as possible he decided to read Mark's Gospel because it was the shortest of the four.

Before he reached the third chapter Anthony suddenly became aware of a presence on the other side of the desk. He was certain that it was Christ who was standing there, and in the weeks and years that followed that certainty never left him. That was the turning point of his life. He had been in the presence of Christ. Therefore he knew that the Gospel story was true. He knew that Jesus Christ had been crucified, and the centurion had been correct when he said, "Truly He is the Son of God."

This personal encounter with the Lord Jesus Christ dispelled all of Anthony's disbelief and transformed his life.

BENIGNO AQUINO   *In solitary*
Leader of the opposition to President   *confinement*
Marcos of the Philippines.
Aquino was assassinated in 1983

When President Marcos declared martial law in the Philippines in 1972 Ninoy Aquino was immediately arrested. In Laur he experienced the deep loneliness of solitary confinement but found that God met with him in a specially profound and real way. Ninoy spent his time meditating on the life of Jesus – His birth to His ascension. Instead of feeling sorry for himself Ninoy met with the living Jesus Christ. He realized that Jesus was the Son of God. He came to see that Jesus was totally innocent of any crime and yet freely gave His life up as a sacrifice for sinners. He was overwhelmed by such thoughts, fell on his knees and begged for Jesus' forgiveness of him.

AN ARCHDEACON

New birth

Story told by Bishop Taylor Smith, who never identified the archdeacon.

The former Chaplain-General of the British Forces, Bishop Taylor Smith, was preaching in a great cathedral. In order to emphasize the necessity of new birth in Christ, he said: "My dear people, do not substitute anything for the new birth. You may be a member of a church, but church membership is not new birth, and 'except a man be born again, he cannot see the kingdom of God'."

He then pointed towards the Archdeacon who sat on his left in his stall and said: "You might even be an Archdeacon like my friend in his stall and not be born again, and 'except a man be born again, he cannot see the kingdom of God'. You might even be a Bishop like myself, and not be born again, and 'except a man be born again, he cannot see the kingdom of God'."

A few days later the Bishop was surprised to receive this letter from the Archdeacon:

"My dear Bishop: You have found me out. I have been a clergyman for over 30 years, but I have never known anything of the joy that Christians speak of. I never could understand it. Mine has been a hard legal service. I did not know what the matter was with me, but when you pointed directly at me, and said, 'You might even be an Archdeacon and not be born again', I realized in a moment what the trouble was. I had never known anything of the new birth."

The next day the Bishop and the Archdeacon met up and spent some time reading the Bible together, after which they knelt down and the Archdeacon acknowledged that he was a sinner and told Christ that he would trust Him as his Saviour.

EDWARD ATKINSON

Disarmed by Christ

Former spiritualist

As an active spiritualist, Atkinson held that "sin" was nothing but a concept which Christians used to browbeat people into their religion. People weren't really bad, he argued – they just didn't understand that after ages of effort they would become part of God.

He hated Christianity. He despised Christians. He scorned Christ. And he put Christ to the test – he challenged Christ to convert him!

The answer to that challenge came gradually. First, Atkinson realized that his claims to righteousness through his own works led to a great deal of self-deception. Then he grew despairing. Then he turned to God – only he did not know what sort of God he was turning to. Then he discovered that non-Christian religions could not satisfy him. He thought he was not so weak that he had to become a Christian – but he found it was already too late to stop Christ entering his life.

"I dodged, I fought, I ran, I hid; but He chased me, held me, disarmed me, and eventually won me. His love triumphed."

The young man who had denounced Christ from spiritualist platforms now took to using those same platforms to denounce spiritualism and proclaim the Christ who was remoulding his life. The old Edward Atkinson had died, but the new man was alive as never before.

AUGUSTINE   *Serenity*
4th-century Bishop of Hippo in North Africa

I threw myself down under a fig tree and collapsed in tears ... "How long, O Lord, how long will you be angry? For ever? Do not hold against us our former sins" [cf. Psalm 79:5–8 and Psalm 85:5] – for I felt I was bound by them ... "Tomorrow and tomorrow? Why not now? Why isn't there an end to my dirtiness here and now?"

I was talking like this and crying with most heartfelt bitterness when I heard a voice (perhaps a child's voice, I'm not sure) coming from a nearby house. It was chanting and repeating the words "Pick it up and read it!" Immediately my face changed and I began seriously to wonder whether children used these words in any of their games, but I couldn't remember ever hearing anything like them. So, subduing my tears, I got up, thinking it must be nothing other than a command from God to open the book and read the first chapter I found. For I had heard that Antony, coming in during the reading of the Gospel, received what was being read as a warning to himself: "Go, sell your possessions and give to the poor, and you will have treasure in heaven. Then come, follow me." [Matthew 19:21] And he was immediately converted to you by this message.

Then I ran back to where Alypius was sitting; for, when I left him, I had left the Apostle's book lying there. I picked it up, opened it, and silently read the passage [Romans 13:13–14] I first set eyes on: "Let us behave decently, as in the daytime, not in orgies and drunkenness, not in sexual immorality and debauchery, not in dissension and jealousy. Rather, clothe yourselves with the Lord Jesus Christ, and do not think about how to gratify the desires of the sinful nature." I didn't want to read any further, and it wasn't necessary. As I reached the end of the sentence, the light of peace seemed to shine on my heart, and every shadow of doubt disappeared.

Confessions, Augustine, Book 8, Section 12

AWI   *"I cannot change!"*
Angolan witch-doctor

When missionaries came to the Tari Valley, old Awi came to watch them. He had served the spirits as local witch-doctor for many years, and if any of his clients asked him about the white men's religion, he would simply say he was too old to think of changing.

After twelve years, however, Awi joined the Enquirers' Class run by the mission, and brought Gugu, his apprentice, with him. There came the day when he announced that he had finished with the old way and was starting a new life as a Christian. He and Gugu were both baptized.

GLADYS AYLWARD
Missionary in China

"God wants you!"

Gladys Aylward attended a Sunday school at a church in Edmonton until she was 14, but then for the next 14 years hardly ever went to church. Her idea of having a good time was to smoke, dance and have a night out with a boy-friend at a theatre if possible.

Her life completely changed when she went along to an evangelistic service at a church in Kensington. The preacher challenged the congregation to commit their lives to Jesus Christ, which was a totally new idea to Gladys.

On the way out of the church the preacher said something to Gladys that she could not get out of her mind: "Miss Aylward, I believe God wants you!" So Gladys later went to the preacher's house and spoke to his wife because he was out. In this peaceful vicarage the two women knelt down side by side and prayed. Gladys gave her life up to God.

GORDON K. BAILEY
Entertainer and evangelist

Six tough hours

Gordon woke his father in the middle of the night after six soul-searching hours. He wanted to pray with him.

During the evening, Gordon's fiancée Corrine had rung him with serious news: she had been to see a Christian film and had committed her life to Jesus Christ!

Now Gordon knew the implications of that. His family had badgered him into a lot of church activity during his childhood, though without succeeding in making him more than a 'pretend Christian'. His friends were Christians, and most of his parents' close friends tried to get him to be a Christian too. Most significant of all, he knew his parents had been praying about the forthcoming marriage of their son to a non-Christian girl. So Gordon knew enough to realize that if Corrine's faith was genuine, she would not think it right to marry an unbeliever.

There was only one answer. Gordon gave in. Praying together with his father, he committed his whole future to Jesus.

PHILIP BAILEY   *Sins washed away*
Lead singer with the band "Earth, Wind and Fire"

Philip Bailey found himself seeking for the meaning of life and looked for this in TM, positive thinking and reading books on Zen. None of these avenues brought him peace of mind. At this time he prayed a simple prayer: if Jesus Christ really was the way to God, would He please reveal Himself to him.

For a year Philip did not see this prayer being answered. But all this changed through an amazing experience which he had in Chicago. He vividly remembers this experience: "The Word of God just pierced my heart and I began to weep uncontrollably."

He knew that Jesus Christ was real and that he was not just having an emotional high. He'd never had any kind of experience like this. It was like "a flushing, that's the only way I can explain it. I felt like my sins had been washed away."

BOBBY BALL   *Brand new start*
Partner in the comedy duo "Cannon and Ball"

Bobby Ball was on the trail of religion. He gave up eating bacon for two years after reading the Old Testament! He searched through a number of religions including Buddhism, and also investigated what some of the sects such as the Mormons and the Jehovah's Witnesses had to offer.

Then Bobby went to see a theatre chaplain, and they had a Bible study together. Bobby told the chaplain how he felt – guilty. The chaplain simply asked Bobby if he had ever turned to Jesus Christ and asked him for his forgiveness. That Bobby did in a prayer with the chaplain, and Bobby dates his conversion from that moment.

THOMAS BARNARDO
Founder of orphanages

No human intervention

I was brought to Christ in the year 1862. A gentleman, a personal friend of mine, a Dr Hunt of Harcourt Street, Dublin, a charming man, had been the means in God's hands of awakening enquiry in the mind of my brother George, who was then at Trinity, of my brother Fred, who was at the school of Medicine ... and of myself a little later on. Eventually my brother Fred's conversion was a great help to me, but I actually found Christ without any human intervention, when alone some few days after a special interview with my brother Fred and Dr Hunt. At this time I was associated with Dr Marrable's congregation at St Werburgh's. He, as you know, was a very earnest Evangelical preacher, a man of great breadth of mind and liberality, especially of prophetic truth, and I continued for many months after my conversion a communicant and member of his congregation and a worker at his meetings.

The Christian, 1903

ROY BARR
Paratrooper

A few words of prayer

Roy Barr, a paratrooper, had no time for God – or for Army Scripture Readers, one of whom had cornered him on leave in Cyprus. This man had only one leg, and had been a prisoner of war under the Japanese, so he deserved some respect, but still religion seemed an irrelevance to Roy.

After a chat during which Roy failed to respond, the Scripture Reader, whose name was Baxter, asked Roy if he'd do him the favour of returning home to meet his wife, who would enjoy meeting someone from home. When they reached the bungalow, it was clear even to Roy that for all their material poverty the Baxters were unutterably content spiritually.

Before leaving, Roy was asked to join the Baxters in "a few

words of prayer". He could hardly refuse, out of politeness, but his mind was on other things. Then he heard Baxter ask: "Do you, Roy Barr, accept Jesus Christ as your personal Saviour?" It seemed a mean trick, but it had put Roy on the spot. In a flash so many thoughts ran through his mind: that he didn't want salvation; that he was a sinner; that he was all right; that he wasn't nearly as all right as the Baxters; that if he did become a Christian he'd probably fail. But he felt that the one word "trust" was being suggested to his mind; so he did. His inner confusion and fear were replaced by a kind of contentment he had not known before, and he felt simply and humbly grateful.

"I do," he stammered.

PHEBE BARTLET
"I can find God now!"
Converted when four years old

She was born in March, in the year 1731. About the latter end of April, 1735, she was greatly affected by the talk of her brother, who had been converted a little before, at about eleven years of age, and then seriously talked to her about the great things of religion. Her parents did not know of it at that time, and were not wont, in the counsels they gave to their children, particularly to direct themselves to her, by reason of her being so young, and as they supposed not capable of understanding: but after her brother had talked to her, they observed her very earnestly to listen to the advice they gave to the other children; and she was observed very constantly to retire several times a day, as was concluded, for secret prayer.

On Thursday, the last day of July, about the middle of the day, the child being in the closet, where it used to retire, its mother heard it speaking aloud "Pray blessed Lord give me Salvation! I pray, beg pardon all my sins!" Her mother then endeavoured to quiet her, and told her she would not have her sad, she must be a good girl, and pray every day, and she hoped God would give her salvation. But this did not quiet her at all; but she continued thus earnestly crying, and talking

4 Finches Park Road
Lindfield West Sussex
RH16 2DN
01444 482540

at the same time, till at length she suddenly ceased crying, and began to smile, and presently said with a smiling countenance, "Mother, the kingdom of heaven is come to me!"

After the child said this, she retired again into her closet; and her mother went over to her brother's, who was next door; and when he came back, the child, being come out of the closet, meets her mother with this cheerful speech, "I can find God now!" Her mother asked her whether she was afraid of going to Hell, and that had made her cry. She answered, "Yes, I was; but now I shan't." Her mother asked her whether she thought that God had given her salvation. She answered "Yes". Her mother asked, "When?" She answered "Today".

A Faithful Narrative of the Surprizing Work of God,
Jonathan Edwards, Oswald, 1737, pp. 109–115

JOHN BERRIDGE   *Mixed covenant*
18th-century vicar of Everton

At the outset of his ministry, Berridge's view of salvation was (he afterwards asserted) like "a solar system without the sun". His failure led him to pray: "Lord, if I am right, keep me so; if I am not right, make me so. Lead me to the knowledge of the truth as it is in Jesus."...

"As I was sitting in my house one morning and musing upon a text of Scripture, the following words were darted into my mind with wonderful power, and seemed like a voice from heaven, viz. 'Cease from thine own works.' Before I heard these words my mind was in a very unusual calm; but as soon as I heard them, my soul was in a tempest directly, and the tears flowed from my eyes like a torrent. The scales fell from my eyes immediately, and I now clearly saw the rock I had been splitting on for near thirty years."

This he elsewhere describes as "the mixed covenant" consisting "*partly* of works and *partly* of grace", with Christ merely thrown in as a makeweight.

He later wrote: "Christ will be either a whole Saviour or none at all. And if you think you have any good service of your own to recommend you to God, you are certainly without any interest in Christ; be ye ever so sober, serious, just and devout, you are still under the curse of God, as I was, and know it not, provided you have allowed reliance on your own works, and think they are doing something for you, and Christ to do the rest ...

"As soon as ever I preached Jesus Christ, and faith in his blood, then believers were added to the Church continually; then people flocked from all parts to hear the glorious sound of the Gospel, some coming six miles, others eight, and others ten, and that constantly."

Works, John Berridge, edited by R. Whittingham, pp. 350–357

DUNCAN BLAIR   *Minesweeping*
Regius Professor of Anatomy
at Glasgow University

Blair grew up with plenty of training in Christianity, yet without actually having the life of Christ in him. He was not satisfied with himself, and knew he was not achieving goodness.

During World War I, he served on board a minesweeper, and after reading the Bible and praying, he realized that if there were indeed a special relationship with Christ into which he ought to enter, then he had better do something about it quickly, for life at that time seemed unusually precarious. And in that moment, he felt that Christ had come to him, that Christ was his goodness, that instead of having constantly prayed to be made into a good person he should have been asking to be made Christ's; and that hitherto he had been disbelieving, while Christ "wanted to be believed in".

JOHN BLANCHARD   *Pass me not*
Evangelist

John Blanchard joined the local Church of England youth club because his stepmother was a Christian and took the two boys to church. He became the club leader and also a Sunday School teacher, but led a double life as a serious gambler.

John fancied a girl in the office where he worked, and accepted her invitation to hear an evangelist. He hated the style of the meeting, which was a world away from Anglican dignity, but in the unfamiliar hymn "Pass me not O gentle Saviour" he sang with meaning the line, "While on others Thou art calling, do not pass me by".

"I didn't go forward," he recalls. "I wasn't counselled, no one followed me up, taught me to do anything or told me I was anything. But I have never doubted that at that moment I was born again. God heard that prayer."

THE BLINCO FAMILY   *All-night prayer*
A colliery fitting-shop foreman and his family

Swearing, drinking, gambling and anger were the features of this godless family in a West Cumberland village shortly after World War II. But Mrs Blinco for some reason went along to a mission service at the Methodist chapel, after a man called at the door with an invitation. That first night saw her converted, and a spiritual opening was created for the rest of the family.

The missioners stayed up all night praying for them, seeing how much they all needed God in their lives. Father and son alike resented the intrusion, but found they could not get away from themselves or from God. The fifteen-year-old son knew he had to set things right between himself and God, and having come to a decision he found it was easy – "He said 'Come' and I came, and I knew He had received me."

Mr Blinco did not go to any of the mission meetings until the very last night, but God must have been working in his heart too because he walked down the aisle and knelt at the communion rail at the end of that last meeting.

PAT BOONE
Singer

Pat Boone became a Christian when he was thirteen and had absolutely no doubt that God existed and expected something of him.

When he went to college, he questioned his faith, but reasoned things through and remained convinced that God was personally interested in him.

For several years, however, he fell away from God, giving up the lifestyle he knew was right even though he continued to go to church. His marriage was deeply shaken because his wife and daughters could see his hypocrisy. "There was little between us except anxieties, animosities and mutual blame," he says.

He knew he needed a miracle, but his church had not encouraged him to believe in miracles. He read *The Cross and the Switchblade*, however, and learned of real miracles taking place in the modern world. He began to talk to God again, and to cry. He asked God to take him, and he experienced a baptism in the Holy Spirit "which was as simple and real an operation as when he saved me".

Family relationships were restored, compromises left behind.

BRAMWELL BOOTH
Son and successor of William Booth

Bramwell Booth writes (in his autobiography, *These Fifty Years*) that when he was a child, "my mother said to me with great tenderness, 'You are very unhappy.' When I replied, 'Yes,' she added, 'You know the reason,' and again I had to say 'Yes.' Then came the clear question as to giving myself to God and I said 'No.' She put her hands suddenly to her face, and I can never forget my feelings on seeing the tears fall through them on to the sawdust beneath our feet. I knew what those tears represented. But still I said 'No.'...

"Sin was revealed in me and I came to see how its power was slowly increasing. My parents treated me with loving patience. They did not say much to me except when alone, and then led my thoughts rather away from myself. I remember, however, how my father's prayers at family worship seemed to take on a new meaning for me."

It was not that little Bramwell was very naughty. But despite his mother's deep desire – not to mention God's desire – he did not want to be religious. He wanted his own way.

Not long afterwards, he went to Walsall with his mother. A mission was being held, over a period of eight weeks, and his mother was leading some meetings for the children. It was in one of these that Bramwell made his decision. His mother did not notice him stand up, but found him at the communion rail with the other children. From the middle of the hall he had made his way there to confess his sin.

As an affectionate and sensitive child, he might well have been misguidedly "helped" with comforting words about God's love, but the young man who was counselling him was led by God to ask the boy what sins he wanted forgiven. Thus Bramwell discovered for himself Christ's power to forgive.

BRIAN BOOTH   *Concern*
Australian test cricketer

Top batsman Brian Booth began playing cricket when he was three, with his dad.

Another thing he did because of his parents was to go to Sunday School and church, although it didn't mean much to him at the time. He stopped going to church as soon as he started living independently, at teacher training college. He lived for his sport.

He passed a church in Sydney and thought he'd go to a service there; and a few days later he met the minister at the local cricket ground. It turned out that he had once played with Brian's own local club. The minister started building on his friendship with the student, inviting him home to suppers and eventually talking to him about belief in Jesus Christ.

He read a verse from the Bible (John 3:16): "For God so loved the world that he gave his one and only Son, that whoever believes in him shall not perish but have eternal life." Brian had heard it before, but was generally very unfamiliar with the Bible. Now, through seeing the minister's concern, he was able to know that God Himself cared for Brian Booth.

WILLIAM BOOTH   *Late at night*
Founder of the Salvation Army

William Booth's name became synonymous with some of the most amazing conversion stories in the pages of the history of Christianity. However, Booth's own conversion was straightforward and unemotional. He was wandering home at about 11 p.m. one night in 1844, when quite suddenly his soul was filled with God's Spirit. It was like Saul's Damascus Road experience. He experienced the light of God's forgiveness in his heart as he confessed his sins. He knew that he was now a follower of the Lord Jesus Christ.

HENRY BOWERS   *At sea*
Member of Scott's last expedition to the Antarctic

Bowers was in the middle of a spiritual struggle within himself when the Lord Jesus Christ Himself intervened. Bowers wrote:

> One night on deck, when things were at their blackest, it seemed to me that Christ came to me and showed me why we are here, and what the purpose of life really is. It is to make a great decision – to chose between the material and the spiritual. While just on the point of choosing the world for good, a possibility which my early training had long kept at bay, Christ revealed Himself to me. Not in a vision; not after hearing emotional preaching, but away at sea. Beside Him, the world at its best was nothing, not even life itself. He filled my whole horizon ... who could

refuse to stick up for such a friend, who even knew him afar off?

It is pretty difficult to express in words what I suddenly saw so plainly, and it is sometimes difficult to recapture it myself. I know too that my powerful ambitions to get on in this world will conflict with that pure light that I saw for a moment, but I can never forget that I did realise, in a flash, that nothing which happens to our bodies really matters.

Bowers always remembered this particular time at sea as the moment when he met with the Lord in a special way. It enabled him, a weak believer, to build on his childhood faith and to make real spiritual progress.

Later he joined Scott's fateful last expedition. Bowers' last letter home to his mother included these words:

> God alone knows what will be the outcome of the 22 miles march we have to make, but my trust is still in Him and in the abounding grace of my Lord and Saviour whom you brought me up to trust in, and who has been my stay through life.

ROBERT BOYLE
17th-century scientist

Thunderstorm

A violent thunderstorm roused him in terror from his sleep, with such loud and frightful peals, attended with flashes of lightning so frequent and dazzling, "that he began to imagine them the sallies of that fire that must consume the world." His apprehension began to prefigure the Day of Judgment to be at hand, while the trembling consciousness of his unprepared condition, led him to the resolution of devoting the remainder of his life, should it be spared, to greater vigilance and attention on the subject of religion. When morning came, and a serene and cloudless sky returned, he renewed and ratified his determination so solemnly, that from that day he dated his conversion.

Nor did his resolutions vanish when the danger was past; for although fear, and he was ashamed to make the confession, was the first occasion of his vow, yet he took care, by his subsequent conduct, to convince the world that he owed not his more deliberate consecration of himself to piety, nor to any less noble motive than that of its own excellence.

Converts from Infidelity, Andrew Critchton, Constable, 1827, vol. ii, pp. 35–36

DAVID BRAINERD   *A new inward view*
Missionary to North American Indians

One morning, while I was walking in a solitary place, as usual, I at once saw that all my contrivances and projections to effect or procure deliverance and salvation for myself were utterly in vain: I was brought entirely to a stand, as finding myself totally lost. Now I saw that I had made all the pleas I ever could have made to all eternity, and all my pleas were vain.

The tumult in my mind was now quieted, and I was eased of that distress which I felt. Before this, the more I did in duty, the more I thought God was obliged to me, or at least the more hard I thought it would be for God to cast me off; though at the same time I confessed, there was no merit in my duties.

But now the more I did in prayer or any other duty, the more I saw I was indebted to God for allowing me to ask for mercy. Now I saw my prayers laid not the least obligation upon God to bestow His grace upon me.

I saw I had been heaping up my devotions before God, fasting, praying. I saw that as I had never done anything for God, I had no claim to anything from Him, but perdition, on account of my hypocrisy and mockery. Oh, how different did not duties now appear from what they used to do!

I continued in this state of mind till the Sabbath evening July 12, 1739, when I was walking again in the same solitary place where I was brought to see myself lost and here was attempting to pray but found no heart to engage in that duty.

My former concern was now gone. I thought the Spirit of God had quite left me, but still was not distressed.

It was a new inward view that I had of God, such as I never

46

had before, nor anything which had the least resemblance to it. I stood still, wondered and admired!

I knew I never had seen before anything comparable to it for excellency and beauty; it was widely different from all the conceptions that ever I had had of God or things divine.

It appeared to be divine glory that I then beheld; and my soul rejoiced with joy unspeakable to see such a glorious Divine Being. I was inwardly pleased and satisfied that He should be God over all for ever and ever.

My soul was so captivated and delighted with the excellency, loveliness, greatness, and other perfections of God, that I was even swallowed up in Him; at least I had no thought about my own salvation.

Thus God brought me to a hearty disposition to exalt Him, and set Him on the throne as King of the universe.

I continued in this state of inward joy and peace till near dark, without any sensible abatement, and then began to think and examine what I had seen, and felt sweetly composed in my mind all the evening following. I felt myself in a new world, and everything about me appeared with the different aspect from what it was wont to do.

At this time, the way of salvation opened to me with such infinite wisdom, suitableness, and excellency, that I wondered I should ever think of any other way. I was amazed that I had not dropped my own contrivances, and complied with this lovely, blessed and excellent way before.

If I could have been saved by my own duties, or any other way that I had formerly contrived, my whole soul would have now refused. I wondered that all the world did not see and comply with this way of salvation, entirely by the righteousness of Christ.

The sweet relish of what I then felt continued with me for several days; I could not but sweetly rejoice in God, lying down and rising up.

But, not long after, I was again involved in thick darkness and under great distress, yet not of the same kind, with my distress under convictions. I was guilty, afraid and ashamed to come before God; was exceedingly pressed with a sense of guilt: but it was not long before I felt true repentance and joy in God.

About August, I again fell under great darkness; it seemed as if the presence of God was clean gone forever; though I was not so much distressed about my spiritual state, as at my being shut out from God's presence. But it pleased the Lord to return graciously to me not long after.

Quoted in *The lives of Brainerd and Fletcher,* Oswald J. Smith, Marshall, Morgan & Scott, 1965, pp. 20–22

WILLIAM BRAMWELL *Consolation lost*
Early Methodist minister

All outward immorality was extremely offensive to him; hence he sometimes followed depraved individuals into public-houses, to dissuade them from their vicious course of life. Mr Brandreth, his master, used to say, "William Bramwell is mad in these things, yet, as a servant, he is inestimable." ... He was also punctual in attendance upon the service of the Parish Church, where he was an early communicant. At this period, the Holy Spirit was in him "a Spirit of bondage to fear;" he found a law in his members warring against the law of his mind, and bringing him into captivity to the law of sin. He used various bodily austerities, in order to overcome the evil propensities of his nature ... His friends therefore consulted two medical gentlemen, who reported his depression of spirits and consequent weakness to be a "nervous complaint".

A short time after this, the Lord in mercy delivered him from the burden and guilt of his sins. He had prepared himself by prayer and self-examination, according to the Rubric of the Church of England, for worthily partaking of the Sacrament of the Lord's Supper; and while in the act of receiving the sacred elements ... obtained the assurance of God's pardoning love. The joy of the Lord then became his strength. His soul was made happy, his bodily health was restored, and he "went on his way rejoicing."

At this period he soon found his need of "the communion

of saints," and suitable instruction in the way of the kingdom. His path was solitary; and, being ignorant of Satan's
devices, ... he lost the consolations of religion, and again
walked in darkness ...

Some time after he had joined the Methodist Society, Mr
Wesley visited Preston, and Mr Bramwell was introduced to
him. Mr Wesley looked attentively at him, and said, "Well,
brother, can you praise God?" Mr Bramwell replied, "No,
Sir." Mr Wesley lifted up his hands, and smiling, said, "Well,
but perhaps you will to-night." Mr Wesley's faith on his
account was realised; for that very night Mr Bramwell found
the comfort he had lost, and was enabled from that time to
walk habitually in the light of God's countenance.

This interview was greatly blessed to Mr Bramwell. The
veteran saint had directed this sincere seeker to "behold the
Lamb of God," and live by faith; he was therefore
strengthened in the ways of the Lord, entered into deeper
communion with God, and became established in the truth.

The Christian Minister in Earnest, Thomas Harris, Wesleyan-Methodist
Book-Room, c.1870, pp. 11–18

COUNT BROBRINSKY
**Russian Minister of the Interior
in the 1870s**

*Through an English
Lord's appeal*

The highly intelligent Count Brobrinsky was annoyed that his
wife had invited Lord Radstock to dinner. Brobrinsky was
very cynical about the reports he had heard of this evangeliz-
ing English Lord and the so-called "drawing-room revival"
that had started as a result of his labours. The Count was
appalled that the English Lord was so ill-mannered as to
expound the theme of the letter to the Romans at the dinner
table. The only religion the Count knew came from a vow he
had made when he had once thought that he was dying. He
had vowed that he would pray a prayer to God every day.
Even though he did not believe in God he still prayed each
day to this Unknown God.

Count Brobrinsky was so certain that he could refute everything that Lord Radstock had said that he left the dinner table when the dessert arrived and went to his study. There he composed a long essay in which he refuted everything that he had heard at the dinner table. The Count was so pleased with his own writing that he even sent it off to be printed. When it returned from the printers he read it but was completely taken by surprise, because he found that his thinking was changed in that moment. In that moment of time he discovered the reality of the eternal Christ for himself. He went down on his knees and humbled himself before Jesus, whom he now knew to be the Unknown God he had formerly prayed to.

JOHN BROWN
18th-century minister of Haddington, Scotland

John 6:64

After a formal slight using of Alleine's *Directions for conversion*, I dedicated myself to the Lord in solemn vow, as Alleine directs (summer 1735 or 1736); particularly, I vowed to pray six times in the day when I was herding, and three when I was not herding; so I continued to do this; and if I was deficient one day, I made amends the next. If I fell into any known sin, I prayed for forgiveness, and so was well. All movings of the affections I took for the special enjoyings of God, and now thought myself sure of heaven, if I was not a hypocrite; to avoid which deceit, I kept the whole of my religion as hid as I could, especially prayer; and to that end prayed almost aye in the field, where, if I was not pretty sure nobody was near, I was exceeding low of voice; and, lest my head being bare might discover it, I cast my blanket over it, or else had an open book before me, that so they might think I was reading; and so made myself, in my conceit, as sure of heaven as possible. In this way of doing I continued from that time till June 1740 or else 1741 at least, if not till now; still putting my fashion of religion in Christ's room, setting up my formal prayers, etc., for my Saviour, yea, for my God ...

At length, after a multitude of ups and downs, glowings of

affections, and sad coolings, I, after a sore fever in 1741, which somewhat awakened my concern about eternal salvation, was providentially determined, during the noontide, while the sheep which I herded rested themselves in the fold, to go and hear a sermon, at the distance of two miles, running both to and from it. The second or third sermon which I heard in this manner, and I had no other opportunity of hearing, the greater part of the year, being preached on John 6:64, "There are some of you that believe not," by one I both before and afterwards reckoned as a most general preacher, pierced my conscience as if almost every sentence had been directed to none but me, and made me conclude myself one of the greatest unbelievers in the world. This sermon threw my soul into no small agony and concern, and made me look on all my former experiences as nothing but common operations of the Spirit; and in this manner I viewed them for many years afterwards; and often in my sermons, after I was a preacher, described the lengths which common operations might go on this footing. But at last I began to doubt that I had been too rash in throwing aside all my former experiences as having nothing of the really gracious in them. And I saw that it was improper for a preacher to make his own experiences, either of one kind or another, anything like a discriminating standard of his conceptions or declarations on these delicate subjects.

John Brown of Haddington, Robert Mackenzie, 1918, pp. 25–26

JOHN BUNYAN
Author of *The Pilgrim's Progress*

Waking dreams

There are some natures to whom the great spiritual world of the unseen is always present as the background of life. It was so with Shakespeare. It was so also with Bunyan, though in a different way. Even when he was a child, the wrong things of the day were followed by the remorse, and fears, and dread dreams of the night. But the real struggle began later, when after his marriage and the reading of his wife's books, he was

51

seen "going to church twice a day, and with the foremost". He had not done this long before there arose a fight with his conscience about Sunday sports, in the course of which there came the weird voices that seemed to be shouted into his ear on Elstow Green.

Somewhere on the sward round the broken pillar of the old Market Cross he was one Sunday in the midst of a game of cat. He had struck it one blow from the hole and was about to strike it the second time, when, as he says, "A voice did suddenly dart from heaven into my soul, which said, Wilt thou leave thy sins and go to heaven, or have thy sins and go to hell? At this I was put to an exceeding maze. Wherefore, leaving my cat upon the ground, I looked up to heaven, and was as if I had with the eyes of my understanding, seen the Lord Jesus looking down upon me, as being very hotly displeased with me." Thus conscience-striken he afterwards made a desperate fling to be rid of conscience altogether, only to find, as other men have, that its grip was tighter than he thought. Then he swung round again and fell to some outward reformation, gave up swearing, took to reading the historical parts of the Bible, and set about keeping the commandments, which he flattered himself he did pretty well; so that in those days he thought he pleased God as well as any man in England. His neighbours were struck with the change, and wondered much to see Mad Tom of Bethlem become a sober man. Their exclamations of surprise flattered his vanity, he became proud of his godliness, and laid himself out for more and more of this kind of incense for about a twelvemonth or more ...

It is dangerous to feel content with one's self; aspiration and not self-complacency is the law of healthful life; and He who was leading Bunyan by a way that he knew not, mercifully shook him out of this unwholesome self-satisfaction. It came about in this way: he saw, as everybody has heard, three or four poor women holding godly talk together as they sat at a door in the sunshine. He had by this time become somewhat of a brisk talker of religion himself; he therefore drew near and listened. He soon found, however, that their talk was above him, and he had to remain silent. They moved in a world of which he knew nothing; they spoke of a holy discontent with themselves and of a new birth from above; they told how God had visited their souls with His love in the Lord Jesus, and with what words and promises they had been refreshed, comforted, and strengthened; they "spake as if joy did make them speak", with such "pleasantness of Scripture language, and with such appearance of grace in all they said", that they seemed to him to have found a new world to which he was altogether a stranger. He was humbled yet fascinated, drawn again and again into their company, and the more he went the more did he question his condition, the more there came over him a "great softness and tenderness of Heart, and a great Bending in his mind" towards godly meditation.

So free from self-consciousness is true life that he in whom faith was beginning to work mightily, now began to wonder whether he had any faith at all. How can he find out? Shall he put it to the test of miracle on the rain pools in the Elstow road? If they should dry up at his word then there would be no doubt. But if not! would not that be proof positive that he "had no Faith, but was a castaway and lost"? It is a great risk to run, too great, "nay, thought I, if it be so, I will never try yet, but will stay a little longer".

Then blossomed into shape his wonderful power of dreaming waking dreams. There were these good people at Bedford sitting on the sunny side of a mountain, while he was separated from them by a wall all about, and shivering in the cold. Round and round that wall he goes to see if there be no opening, be it ever so narrow, and at last he finds one. But it is narrow, indeed so narrow that none can get through but those who are in downright earnest, and who leave the wicked world behind them. There is just room for body and soul, but not for body and soul and sin. It must be a strait gate through which a man gets rid of self; but by dint of sidling and striving he first gets in his head, then his shoulders, and then his whole body, at which he is exceeding glad, for now too he is in the sunshine and is comforted. But as yet this is only in a dream, and dreams tarry not. This man who was an elect soul, if ever there was one – elect through suffering to help other souls – begins to torment himself as to whether he is elect or not. Perhaps he is not. How if the day of grace be past and gone, and he has overstood the time of mercy? Oh, would that he had turned sooner! would he had turned seven years ago! Words cannot tell with what longings and breakings of soul he cried to heaven to call him, little thinking that the longings and breakings themselves were the very call for which he cried. Gold! Could this blessing be gotten for gold, what would he have given for it? For this the whole world would have gone ten thousand times over, if he had only had it. Meantime that very world went on its old way. How strange that it should; how strange that people should go hunting after perishable things with eternal things before them, that even Christian people should make so much of mere outward losses! If his soul were only right with God, and he could but be sure that it was, he should count himself rich with nothing but bread and water.

Strange alternatives of gloom and glory came over him. Sometimes his soul was visited with such visions of light and hope that he could have spoken of God's love and mercy to the very cows on the ploughed land before him. He thought then that he should never forget that joy even in forty years' time, but alas! in less than forty days the vision was all faded and gone. Worse than gone, for there now came down upon him a great storm of conflict which handled him twenty times worse than before. Star after star died out of the firmament of his hope; darkness seized upon him, and to his amazement and confusion a whole flood of doubts and blasphemies poured in upon his spirit. They seemed to be coming in from morning to night, and to be carrying him away as with a mighty whirlwind.

Yet even in that dark time of despair there was this redeeming gleam of hope, that while dreadful things were pouring into his soul, there was something within him that refused to tolerate them. If he is borne along, he goes struggling and crying for deliverance, like the child some gipsy is carrying off by force and fraud from friend and country. A man is safe so long as the citadel of his own will is kept. There is the turning point of destiny – the centre of life's mystery. And all was right there. Floods of temptation came dashing against the outworks, but within he had, he says, great yearnings after God, and heart-affecting apprehensions of Him and His truth. So that he really was making way, getting out of himself more and on to the solid ground of divine fact. There began to come to him such words as these, "If God be for us, who can be against us?" and these, "He hath made peace by the blood of His cross."

Fortunately too for him, some time before this the good people at Bedford had taken him to hear Mr Gifford, their minister. Under his teaching how was his soul led on from truth to truth by the Spirit of Truth! Even from the birth and cradle of the Son of God to His ascension and second coming, he was "orderly led" into the gospel story; and so vivid was everything that it seemed to him as if he had actually seen Christ born and grow up, seen Him walk through the world from the cradle to the cross, he actually leaped at the grave's mouth for joy that Christ was risen again, had actually, in spirit, seen Him at the right hand of the Father, and that on his behalf.

At this stage of his experience also it was his hap to light upon an old book, a book so old that it was ready to fall to pieces in his hand if he did but turn it over. Yet never was gold more precious. For he found his own conditions so largely and profoundly handled in it, as if it had been written out of his own heart. It was a copy of the "Commentary on the Galatians," by Martin Luther, perhaps the one man of all the centuries most fitted to walk with Bunyan along that path of his journey which lay through the valley of the shadow of death. Bunyan, like his own Christian, "thought he heard the voice of a man going before him". Grateful indeed was he for that, "This, me thinks, I must let fall before all men. I do prefer this book of Martin Luther (excepting the Holy Bible) before all books that ever I have seen as most fit for a wounded conscience."... [Luther's commentary on Galatians]

He remembered long years afterwards how at this dark time he went one day into Bedford and, spent and weary, sat down upon a settle in the street. It seemed to him then as if the very sun in the heavens did grudge to give him light, as if the very stones in the street and the tiles upon the houses did bend themselves against him. "O how happy now was every creature over I was! for they stood and kept fast their station, but I was gone and lost." The worst, however, was now past, and daylight was near. As if in echo to his own self-reproaches a voice seemed to say to him, "This sin is not unto death." He wondered at the fitness and the unexpectedness of the sentence thus shot into his soul. The "power and sweetness and light and glory that came with it also were marvellous." Then again one night as he retired to rest there came to him the quieting assurance: "I have loved thee with an everlasting love," and next morning it was still fresh upon his soul. Again when doubts came as to whether the blood of Christ was sufficient to save him, there came also the words, "He is able." "Methought this word *able* was spoke loud unto me – it showed a great word, it seemed to be writ in great letters." One day as he was passing into the field, still with some fears in his heart, suddenly this sentence fell into his soul, "'Thy righteousness is in heaven': and methought withal I saw with the eye of my soul, Jesus Christ at God's right hand. I saw, moreover, that it was not my good frame of heart that made my righteousness better, nor yet my bad frame that made my righteousness worse; for my righteousness was Jesus Christ Himself, the same yesterday, to-day, and for ever. Now did my chains fall from my legs indeed; I was loosed from my afflictions and irons. Oh, methought, Christ! Christ! there was nothing but Christ that was before my eyes! I could look from myself to Him and should reckon that all those graces of God that now were green on me, were yet but like those crack-groats and fourpence halfpennies that rich men carry in their purses, when their gold is in their trunks at home! Oh, I saw my gold was in my trunk at home! In Christ my Lord and Saviour! Now Christ was all; all my wisdom, all my righteousness, all my sanctification, and all my redemption!"

John Bunyan, John Brown, Isbister, 1885, pp. 62–68

John Calvin was born on July 10th, 1509, at Noyon in north-
ern France. By the time that he had become a student at Paris,
the Protestant Reformation was under way in Germany and
the ripples were reaching Paris. Some time in the early 1530s,
"God by a sudden conversion subdued and brought my mind
to a teachable frame," as Calvin himself put it. His conversion occurred in 1533 when he was twenty-four. He
described it briefly in the preface to his *Commentary on the
Psalms* and compares David's struggles with his own. Here is
what Calvin says:

> It is true that my estate is much humbler and lower than David's
> ... but as he was taken from caring for beasts and raised to the
> sovereign rank of royal dignity, so God has advanced me from
> my lowly and humble beginnings so far as to call me to this most
> honourable office of minister and preacher of the Gospel. From
> the time that I was a young child my father had intended me for
> theology; but afterwards, because he perceived that the science of
> laws commonly enriches those who follow it, this hope caused
> him promptly to change his plan. That was the reason why I was
> withdrawn from the study of philosophy, and why I was set to
> learning law. Though I forced myself to engage faithfully in it in
> order to obey my father, God finally made me turn about in
> another direction by his secret providence.
>   And, in the first place, because I was so obstinately addicted to
> the superstitions of the papacy that it was very hard to draw me
> from that deep slough, *by a sudden conversion He subdued and
> reduced my heart to docility.* Having consequently received some
> taste and knowledge of true piety, I was forthwith inflamed with
> so great a desire to reap benefit from it that although I did not at
> all abandon other studies, yet I devoted myself to them more
> indifferently.

His conversion was to the service of Jesus Christ and, in
particular, to the Protestant cause. As a result, he had to leave
France in 1534, because of the fierce campaign of persecution
which was launched against the Protestants. Calvin withdrew
to Basel, in Switzerland, where he hoped to lead the quiet life
of a scholar and writer. But in August 1536 he was forced by

circumstances to stop overnight at Geneva. William Farel, who had recently introduced the Reformation into Geneva, saw Calvin's potential and bullied him into staying as a Bible teacher.

The Institutes of Christian Religion, John Calvin, edited by Tony Lane and Hilary Osborne, Hodder & Stoughton, 1986, p. 11

STEVE CAMP *Going through the motions*
Christian musician

Steve became a Christian when he was five, but it was not until he was 17 that God really took over his life. His father had died of a heart attack, his younger brother had died in a motorcycle accident, and Steve faced God.

He had grown up in the United States, in a Christian family, but had found that much of Christianity was just a watered-down, official religion. What people really respond to, he feels, is somebody who's "real" – it might be a musician – and many people do not see much that is "real" in the churches.

Steve has recognized how important it is for young people to be able to question things, to get angry at the establishment – provided they can talk about it openly and deal with it in the light of Jesus Christ.

GEORGE CAREY *Shamayim, Shamayim, Shamayim*
Archbishop of Canterbury

George Carey says that he was converted when he was seventeen. Twenty years later he was lecturing in an evangelical Anglican theological college and was by that time particularly upset about his lack of spirituality. He goes so far as to say that he experienced a "spiritual void or *ennui*". This came into sharp focus when he was lecturing on St Paul's doctrine of the Spirit. He became acutely aware of the great gulf between Paul's triumphant assurance and his own "spiritual poverty".

Things changed for George Carey in Canada. He read a book called *Aglow with the Spirit* by Robert Frost just before he was due to preach in Little Trinity Church, Toronto. He recalls that he unexpectedly found himself on his knees. He told his Lord that he had been so busy in serving Him that he had somehow lost Him. He asked to be filled again with God's Spirit. He knew that without this he could not go on.

Carey recalls that nothing special happened immediately after this except that he kept on hearing the word *Shamayim* repeated. It is the Hebrew word for "heaven". Later Carey understood that what he had experienced that evening was a foretaste of heaven as the Holy Spirit had become so real to him.

He felt that this experience was a turning point in his Christian life. Dying embers had been fanned by God's Spirit into a fire. He could now move on again.

WILLIAM CAREY
Missionary in India

Day of prayer

Carey was apprenticed to a shoemaker, along with Thomas Warr. They would often start arguing about their different views about Christian doctrine. Carey was good with words, and could easily out-argue the less bookish Warr, but he found he got no lasting enjoyment from his victories. His fellow's faith was real faith, and Carey knew it was a different thing from his own.

In 1779 the war with America was continuing and England was also at war with France and Spain. It was a difficult time for the nation. English soldiers were even fighting in India. At home, there were divisions within families and people were altogether unhappy with the state of politics. A National Day of Prayer was called.

Carey and Warr together went to join the prayer meeting in the small meeting-room of the local Dissenting congregation. One of the members read Hebrews 13:13: "Let us go forth therefore unto him without the camp, bearing his reproach."

The words were familiar to William, but now they found a deep resonance in his heart. The world was still rejecting Christ, but William knew that he had to commit himself, not intellectually but with his heart. It came as the climax of several weeks of searching, and he realized that at last Christ had found him and given him peace.

JIMMY CARTER   *Baptist background*
Former President of the United States

Carter's Christian experiences are rooted in his Baptist background. He was baptized by immersion in 1935, although, he admits, his new birth came to him later on in life. Talking of the period 1963–1965 he once said, "I never did have a personal feeling of intimacy with Christ until, I'd say, ten, twelve years ago, and then I began to see much more clearly the significance of Christ in my life, and it changed my attitudes dramatically."

Since the 1970s Carter has been saying, "My religion is as natural to me as breathing," and "the most important thing in my life beyond all else is Jesus Christ".

GEORGE WASHINGTON CARVER   *A ten-year-old*
Discoverer of over 300 peanut products

The botanist George Washington Carver (d. 1943) was unquestionably one of the most influential men of his day and has even been rated as "arguably the most remarkable American who ever lived". His start in life could hardly have been less auspicious, as he was born a black slave without a name on an unrecorded date. Against overwhelming odds he became the most celebrated 20th-century American botanist as he worked on making the peanut into a marketable product.

He had a very simple conversion. Even at the age of ten Carver knew that he was a slave who had no power or status in the world. He was delighted to trust God and receive solace and friendship from Jesus Christ.

He wrote the following about his conversion: "God came into my heart one afternoon while I was alone in the loft of our big barn. That was my simple conversion, and I have tried to keep the faith." George just knelt down on a barrel of corn and prayed to God as well as he was able.

JOHN CENNICK *Overwhelmed with joy*
The first Methodist lay preacher

Cennick came from a religious family but rebelled in his teens, taking up with undesirable companions and indulging worldly tastes. "I had forgotten Jesus," he admitted. Becoming conscious of his sin, however, he spent a period searching spiritually, and was converted when he was 19. He tells us that he struggled in vain against the compelling power of the Holy Spirit; he felt so low that he prayed for death. He tried to get out of this slough by self-discipline, but failed.

Then, at an ordinary church service, the appointed psalm was sung: "Great are the troubles of the righteous, but the Lord delivereth him out of them all; and they that put their trust in him shall not be destitute" (Psalm 34). The singing stopped, and Cennick found himself overwhelmed with joy. "I believed there was mercy ... I rejoiced in God my Saviour." He continued his work as a surveyor but his life had taken on new meaning.

At Bristol, where he had gone to see the site of Wesley's new school, he found a crowd assembled waiting for a preacher who had not turned up. Cennick was urged, against his cautious judgement, to preach to them. "The burden of the Lord came upon me," he reported later, "and I began to open my mouth to testify of Jesus Christ. The Lord bore witness with my words, insomuch that many believed in that hour."

Wesley made him his first lay preacher, but after a time he severed his connections with Methodism (being careful to

ensure there were no hard feelings about it) and devoted himself to evangelistic work in Wiltshire, under the aegis of the
Moravian church.

MARGARET CHARLTON   *Self-judging*
Later to become the wife of the Puritan
minister Richard Baxter

She heard a sermon ... upon that text, Isaiah 27:11. "It is a
people of no understanding, therefore he that made them will
not save them," etc. This wrought much upon her, and the
doctrine of conversion, preached by Mr Baxter, and afterwards printed by him, in his Treatise of Conversion, was
received on her heart, as a seal on the wax. Whereupon she
presently fell to self-judging, frequent reading, and prayer,
and serious thoughts about her present and future estate ...

All her religious friends, and neighbours, rejoiced much,
and praised God for so sudden and great a change ...

These convictions did neither die, nor drave her into despair:
but, through God's mercy, grew up to serious conversion ...

Yet she continued under great fears that she had not saving
grace, because she had not that degree of holy affections
which her soul longed after ...

After her marriage her sadness and melancholy vanished
away, for advice and counsel contributed towards the cure of
it, as did content, and employment about household affairs;
and with her husband she lived in inviolable love, and mutual
complacency ...

The Lives of Sundry Eminent Persons in this Later Age, Samuel Clarke, Simmons,
1683, pp. 182–185 of the last section

FREDERICK CHARRINGTON   *John chapter 3*
Brewer's son

At the end of a continental holiday together, a friend asked
Frederick Charrington if he was saved. Young Fred found
this a distasteful and inappropriate subject, and tried to turn

the conversation back to their reminiscences about the holiday, but eventually he agreed to read the third chapter of John's Gospel.

As he read, he realized that this was the second of his friends who had directed him to that same chapter, believing that they were "saved". He wrote: "as I read the chapter, light came into my soul, and as I came to the words, 'He that believeth on the Son hath everlasting life' I realized that I, too, possessed the 'eternal life'".

He had previously thought of "conversion" as something hysterical, leaving no lasting result, but he came to see this unhysterical moment as the turning-point in his life. There was little emotion, little outward change at the time, but there was a real and lasting interior change which led him at a later date to abandon his family brewery business with all its wealth, and choose a path which he was more able to square with his social conscience.

ELDRIDGE CLEAVER
Black American Marxist revolutionary leader in the 1960s

Man in the moon

Whilst living in France to escape the US police, Eldridge Cleaver was downcast and moody. He looked up at the moon one night and studied the shadows. He thought he saw the face of the "man in the moon", and then he thought it was himself in profile. He began to shake uncontrollably, from deep down within him, until he felt he might collapse and disappear. He continued to look at the moon, and fancied the picture changed to the faces of the heroes he had looked up to: Castro, Mao, Marx and Engels appeared, one after another. Finally, in a bright light, he found he was looking at Jesus.

Cleaver sobbed. He knelt and held on to the stair-rail and found himself repeating the Lord's Prayer and Psalm 23, which seemed to calm him a little. As he got more in control of himself he reached for a Bible.

After a night of peaceful sleep, he woke suddenly, as though he had been woken at someone's prompting, and he felt sure of the way back home. He did not need to wait for politicians' help; it was up to him to surrender, knowing that everything would work out all right.

NATHAN COLE   *Whitefield's preaching*
18th-century farmer in Connecticut

When I was young I had very early convictions; but after I grew up I intended to be saved by my own works.

There came a messenger and said Mr Whitefield is to preach at Middletown this morning at ten of the clock. I was in my field at work, I dropped my tool that I had in my hand and ran home to my wife telling her to make ready quickly ... then ran to my pasture for my horse with all my might ... I with my wife soon mounted the horse and went forward as fast as I thought the horse could bear.

My hearing him preach, gave me a heart wound; by God's blessing, my old foundation was broken up, and I saw that my righteousness would not save me.

I went month after month mourning and begging for mercy, I tryed every way I could think to help my self and all ways failed.

I made great resolutions that I would forsake every thing that was sinful. And at once I felt a calm in my mind. I began to think I was converted, for I thought I felt a real change in me, but in the space of ten days, my convictions came on again.

I told my mother I was going right down to hell, for I cannot feel grieved for my self, I can't relent, I can't weep for myself, I cannot shed one tear for my sins. I cannot pray, my heart is as hard as stone.

God appeared unto me and he seemed to speak to me in an angry and sovereign way: "What, won't you trust your soul with God?" My heart answered, "O yes, yes, yes."

Then I was set free, my distress was gone, and I was filled

with a pining desire to see Christ's own words in the Bible. Then I began to pray and to praise God.

Then I saw what an abominable unbeliever I had been. I had true mourning for sin. Now my heart talked with God; now everything praised God.

Spiritual Travels, Nathan Cole

CHARLES COLSON   *"Take me"*
Adviser to President Nixon,
imprisoned after the Watergate trial

Colson was racked with doubts about Christianity. He could not get the phrase "Jesus Christ is God" out of his head. In the best way he knew he had surrendered to God and asked Him to take him. However, he had no certainty about his faith and he spent the next week studying the Bible. During this time he felt as if he made massive spiritual progress in his understanding about Christianity. Then he was able to articulate a prayer which he had thought would never pass his lips. He told Jesus that he believed in Him, and accepted Him. He asked Jesus to come into his life, and he committed his life to his Lord.

Colson immediately had a sense of God's comfort and the knowledge that he could now face life with Christ in a totally new and reformed way.

Charles Colson now knew what it was to be born again in Christ.

NORTON COLVILLE   *A group of young people*
Dance teacher and band leader

St John's Wood Underground station in London, 2 p.m. on a Saturday in 1956: Norton Colville has to give a dancing lesson at 4 p.m. and is on his way to spend the intervening time in St Martin-in-the-Fields parish church, where he has gone for a time every day for ten months.

At the church he hears a group of young people singing about Jesus, and gets talking to one of them. The young man offers him a leaflet called *What do you think of Christ?* and Colville's answer is, "I really don't know, but I think I have been trying to find him."

A conversation begins, which leads to Colville giving his life to Christ and leaving St Martin's with inner assurance that he has been pardoned.

CORNELIUS   *Preaching to the Gentiles*
1st-century Roman centurion

At Caesarea there was a man named Cornelius, a centurion in what was known as the Italian Regiment. He and all his family were devout and God-fearing; he gave generously to those in need and prayed to God regularly. One day at about three in the afternoon he had a vision. He distinctly saw an angel of God, who came to him and said, "Cornelius!"

Cornelius stared at him in fear. "What is it, Lord?" he asked.

The angel answered, "Your prayers and gifts to the poor have come up as a memorial offering before God. Now send men to Joppa to bring back a man named Simon who is called Peter. He is staying with Simon the tanner, whose house is by the sea."

When the angel who spoke to him had gone, Cornelius called two of his servants and one of his soldiers who was a devout man. He told them everything that had happened and sent them to Joppa.

About noon the following day as they were approaching the city, Peter went up on the roof to pray. He became hungry and wanted something to eat, and while the meal was being prepared, he fell into a trance. He saw heaven opened and something like a large sheet being let down to earth by its four corners. It contained all kinds of four-footed animals, as well as reptiles of the earth and birds of the air. Then a voice told him, "Get up, Peter. Kill and eat."

"Surely not, Lord!" Peter replied. "I have never eaten anything impure or unclean."

The voice spoke to him a second time, "Do not call anything impure that God has made clean."

This happened three times, and immediately the sheet was taken back to heaven.

While Peter was wondering about the meaning of the vision, the men sent by Cornelius found out where Simon's house was and stopped at the gate. They called out, asking if Simon who was known as Peter was staying there.

While Peter was still thinking about the vision, the Spirit said to him, "Simon, three men are looking for you. So get up and go downstairs. Do not hesitate to go with them, for I have sent them."

Peter went down and said to the men, "I'm the one you're looking for. Why have you come?"

The men replied, "We have come from Cornelius the centurion. He is a righteous and God-fearing man, who is respected by all the Jewish people. A holy angel told him to have you come to his house so that he could hear what you have to say." Then Peter invited the men into the house to be his guests.

The next day Peter started out with them, and some of the brothers from Joppa went along. The following day he arrived in Caesarea. Cornelius was expecting them and had called together his relatives and close friends. As Peter entered the house, Cornelius met him and fell at his feet in reverence. But Peter made him get up. "Stand up," he said, "I am only a man myself."

Talking with him, Peter went inside and found a large gathering of people. He said to them: "You are well aware that it is against our law for a Jew to associate with a Gentile or visit him. But God has shown me that I should not call any man impure or unclean. So when I was sent for, I came without raising any objection. May I ask why you sent for me?"

Cornelius answered: "Four days ago I was in my house praying at this hour, at three in the afternoon. Suddenly a man in shining clothes stood before me and said, 'Cornelius,

God has heard your prayer and remembered your gifts to the poor. Send to Joppa for Simon who is called Peter. He is a guest in the home of Simon the tanner, who lives by the sea.' So I sent for you immediately, and it was good of you to come. Now we are all here in the presence of God to listen to everything the Lord has commanded you to tell us."

Then Peter began to speak: "I now realise how true it is that God does not show favouritism but accepts men from every nation who fear him and do what is right. This is the message God sent to the people of Israel, telling the good news of peace through Jesus Christ, who is Lord of all. You know what has happened throughout Judea, beginning in Galilee after the baptism that John preached – how God anointed Jesus of Nazareth with the Holy Spirit and power, and how he went around doing good and healing all who were under the power of the devil, because God was with him.

"We are witnesses of everything he did in the country of the Jews and in Jerusalem. They killed him by hanging him on a tree, but God raised him from the dead on the third day and caused him to be seen. He was not seen by all the people, but by witnesses whom God had already chosen – by us who ate and drank with him after he rose from the dead. He commanded us to preach to the people and to testify that he is the one whom God appointed as judge of the living and the dead. All the prophets testify about him that everyone who believes in him receives forgiveness of sins through his name."

While Peter was still speaking these words, the Holy Spirit came on all who heard the message. The circumcised believers who had come with Peter were astonished that the gift of the Holy Spirit had been poured out even on the Gentiles. For they heard them speaking in tongues and praising God.

Then Peter said, "Can anyone keep these people from being baptised with water? They have received the Holy Spirit just as we have." So he ordered that they be baptised in the name of Jesus Christ. Then they asked Peter to stay with them for a few days.

Acts 10:1–48

G. C. COSSAR

1 out of 3,000

**Scottish doctor and leader of Boys' Clubs
in Scotland and Canada**

Despite a Presbyterian upbringing and a truly Christian and
prayerful mother, Dr Cossar's own Christianity was more an
intellectual than a personal knowledge. In America, where he
had even had some contact with spiritualists, he went to a
mission and was the only person, out of 3,000 present, who
stood up when the speaker asked if there was any sinner who
desired the prayers of the meeting.

Critical circumstances conspired together very shortly
afterwards, at which time his mother back in Scotland had a
vision of the crisis and was led to get up in the early morning
to pray for her son.

When he returned home, he talked at length to his mother
about the eternal dimension to life and prayed to Christ to
accept him as a sinner. The next morning he knew he was
different, and that he had been reconciled to God. Later he
was also filled with the Holy Spirit, and so was enabled to
win others for Christ.

JOHN COTTON

Tolling bell

17th-century Puritan preacher

During his residence in the university, God began to work
upon him by the ministry of Mr William Perkins of blessed
memory: but the motions, and stirrings of his heart which
then were, he suppressed, thinking that if he should trouble
himself with matters of religion, according to the light he had
then received, it would be an hindrance to him in his studies,
which then he had much addicted himself unto. Therefore he
was willing to silence those suggestions, and inward callings
which he had from God's Spirit, and did wittingly defer the
prosecution of that work until afterwards. At length, as he
was walking in the fields, he heard the bell tolling for Mr Perkins, who lay a dying, whereupon he was secretly glad in his
heart, that he should now be rid of him, who had (as he said)

laid siege to, and beleaguered his heart. This became matter of much affliction to him afterwards, God keeping it upon his spirit, with the aggravation of it, and making it an effectual means of convincing, and humbling him in the sight, and sense of the natural enmity that is in man's nature against God. Afterwards hearing Dr Sibbes (then Mr Sibbes) preaching a sermon about regeneration, wherein he shewed, first, what regeneration was not, and so opening the state of a mere civil man. Mr Cotton saw his own condition fully discovered, which (through God's mercy) did drive him to a stand, as plainly seeing himself, destitute of true grace, all his false hopes, and grounds now failing him: and so he lay for a long time, in an uncomfortable despairing way: and of all other things this was his heaviest burden, that he had wittingly withstood the means, and offers of grace and mercy which he found had been tendered to him; thus he continued till it pleased God to let in a word of faith into his heart, and to cause him to look unto Christ for his healing, which word also was dispersed unto him by the same Dr Sibbes, which begat in him a singular, and constant love to the said doctor, of whom he was also answerably beloved.

A Collection of the Lives of Ten Eminent Divines, Samuel Clarke, 1662, pp. 57–58

COLIN COWDREY   *Challenge*
English test cricketer

Brought up in a church-going family, Colin Cowdrey accepted church as part of life's normal routine in much the same way as eating, working or playing were part of life's routine. Not until he was in his mid teens and preparing for confirmation did he consciously think about Christianity. Then he realized that it was a personal relationship with God.

As a Christian, he came to see each day as dedicated to God, to be lived in humble dependence on the Holy Spirit. He felt sorry for those people who never faced the challenge of faith in Christ but treated the Gospel story as they might a work of art or a story from secular history.

WILLIAM COWPER   *A Bible found*
18th-century English poet and hymn-writer

In July 1764, Cowper found a Bible lying on a bench in his
garden, and opened it at John chapter 11. He began to turn
the pages and eventually came to Romans 3:25: "Whom God
set forth to be a propitiation through faith in His blood."
Light flooded his mind. He believed and received the Gospel.

WENDY CRAIG   *Through the death of her dog*
British actress

Wendy Craig grew up in the love and happiness of a Christian family and loved to say prayers herself. As she grew older
she didn't feel so much need for God and drifted away from
Him.

Wendy's conversion was strongly linked to her English set-
ter, Tallis, whom she loved with all her heart. One night she
was awakened by some strange noises. It was Tallis – clearly
he was ill. He had tried to climb the stairs but had fallen back
and lay dying on the floor. Wendy cuddled and comforted
him, and he died in her arms. Through this sad experience she
became depressed and found herself wandering into a church
one day. In the church she prayed and asked God to forgive
her for assuming that she could manage her own life without
His divine help. She felt genuine sadness for this sin of hers
and experienced God's wonderful forgiveness then and there.
Wendy marks that moment as the time when she became a
real Christian.

RICHARD CREED   *Independent and dependent*
Spastic

If only he could walk, thought the English boy Richard
Creed, there would be no problem. But he was confined to a
wheel-chair, and he deeply resented it.

After leaving school, he started work in his father's shop, and started going to a church where people took a personal interest in him. He learned that what he needed was not a changed body but a changed heart. To be as independent as possible physically was good, but he had to learn to be spiritually dependent on God. Through a Tom Rees mission, God removed Richard's feelings of bitterness and frustration; the feeling that the wheel-chair was an encumbrance was changed in to a recognition that it could be a means whereby Richard could meet people and help them learn more about God's love.

OLIVER CROMWELL
17th-century English revolutionary leader

"I loved darkness and hated the light"

Cromwell's family doctor, Dr Simcott, is a mine of information about the character of Oliver Cromwell. Dr Simcott claims that Cromwell took mithridate, an antidote to poison, to protect himself against the plague and found a cure for the pimples on his face in the process. Sometimes Dr Simcott would be sent for in the small hours of the morning because Cromwell was feeling "melancholy" or that he would die because of the thoughts that his vivid imagination was giving him. He once thought that he could see a huge cross standing in the middle of Huntingdon. On another occasion Cromwell told Dr Simcott that he had a vision of being the greatest man in the kingdom.

Cromwell reveals the state of his soul in a letter he wrote to his cousin Mrs St John in 1638.

I honour my God by declaring what He hath done for my soul. The Lord accepts me in His Son, and gives me to walk in the light as He is the light. He it is that enlighteneth our blackness, our darkness. I dare not say, He hideth His face from me. He giveth me to see light in His light. One beam in a dark place hath exceeding much refreshment in it. Blessed be His Name for shining upon so dark a heart as mine! You know what my manner of life hath been. Oh, I have lived in and loved darkness and hated the light. I was a chief, the chief of sinners. This is true; I hated godliness, yet God had mercy on me. O the riches of His mercy! Praise Him for me, that He hath begun a good work should perfect it to the day of Christ.

Letters, Oliver Cromwell, c.1645

GARTH CROOKS
British footballer and journalist

"Know that I am God"

Garth Crooks scored 129 goals in 375 appearances in League football matches and was Chairman of the Professional Footballers' Association from 1988 to 1990.

Garth's mum used to read Bible stories to the children, and sent them to a church school. But the turning-point for him came after he had become a professional footballer. He used to speak to God at great length, blaming Him for all sorts of things.

"This happened for about six months and then I felt God say, 'When you are ready to listen to what I've got to say, you'll shut up and I'll begin to talk!'" God had allowed him to do what he wanted, but never had Garth asked God whether He approved.

Thanks to friendships with people like the rock singer David Grant, he went one Sunday to Kensington Temple, a charismatic church in London, where "they seemed to put as much into the worship as I put into football". During Pastor Wynne Lewis' sermon Garth realized his own insignificance. He had been treating God as if He was on a level with his own casual friends. He apologized to God, and felt God's reply: "Know that I am God."

Garth started going to church regularly, and began to live his life according to God's demands.

**Former teenage gang leader in New York,
now an evangelist**

When David Wilkerson, a local preacher, offered to shake
hands with Nicky Cruz, the vicious gang leader slapped him
across the cheek and spat in his face.

Wilkerson was unwilling to give up with Cruz and told him
that the Roman soldiers had spat on Christ as well, but He
had prayed for them as they nailed him to the cross, "Father,
forgive them, for they do not know what they are doing."

This only made Nicky curse and shout louder still.

As he went away Wilkerson left three words ringing in the
ears of the much-feared Mau Mau gang leader: "Jesus loves
you."

Nicky was bugged by those three words. He could not stop
thinking, "Jesus loves you."

Wilkerson invited Cruz's gang to a meeting the following
week. Cruz had decided that he would not go along until one
of his gang teased him and said he was "chicken" if he was
scared to face a skinny preacher.

The Mau Mau gang turned up in force to Wilkerson's
meeting and took great delight in disrupting it. Although
Cruz was not able to hear a great deal of what Wilkerson was
saying, his terrible deeds flashed through his mind and he
began to experience genuine sorrow for them.

Then he heard Wilkerson's words, "If you want your life
changed, now is the time. Stand up! Those who want Jesus
Christ to save them from their sins and to be changed, stand
up! Come forward!"

Nicky went forward, as did more than 20 other Mau Maus
and about 30 boys from other gangs.

CYPRIAN
3rd-century theologian

A slave to sin

Cyprian, a wealthy Carthaginian, knew that, for all his superficial suavity, he was sinful. In a letter he wrote:

> I used to wander blindly in the darkness of night, buffeted this way and that in the stormy sea of the world; I floated to and fro, ignorant of my own life, and a stranger to the truth and the light. Given the manner of life I lived in those days, I used to think that what God in his tenderness promised me for my salvation was difficult, indeed distasteful. How could a man be reborn and quickened for a new life in the water of baptism? How could one be regenerated and have done with all the past, and, without physical changes, be altered in heart and soul? How, I asked myself, was such a conversion possible? For I was captured and held prisoner by the countless sins of my past life; I did not believe it was possible to be rid of them. So I became a slave to my vices. I despaired of better things. I learned to make excuses for my faults which had become my familiar friends.

When he was baptized, he found Christ's forgiveness, and the Holy Spirit's transforming power. Later he wrote of this experience:

> The water of regeneration washed away the stains of my past life. A light from above entered and permeated my heart, now cleansed from its defilement. The Spirit came from heaven, and changed me into a new man by the second birth. Almost at once in a marvellous way doubt gave way to assurance; what had been shut tight, opened; light shone in dark places; and I found what had previously seemed difficult had become easy, and what I had thought impossible could be done.

DANA
Irish winner of the Eurovision Song Contest

In a prayer group

Dana (whose real name is Rosemary Brown) won the Eurovision Song Contest for Ireland in 1970 with the song "All Kinds of Everything". She has had one great religious experience that transformed her life. Before this experience, she says, she had been rather lukewarm about God.

Then she found herself in a small prayer group and everybody was praying out loud. She particularly remembers a nun and a priest being present. Then they prayed over Dana herself and she felt an inexplicable feeling of being loved by God down in the centre of her being. It was a kind of love that she had never been aware of before and was unlike any human love. She now felt that she had met with God Himself.

PETER J. DANIELS   *"The message seemed*
Australian businessman   *to be for me."*

In 1959 Peter and Robina Daniels were given tickets for a Billy Graham crusade. Dr Graham was an American, and the Daniels thought about the friendly GI's who had been in Australia in World War II.

The crusade meeting took Peter by surprise. "Something was happening," he says, "and I couldn't understand it. As I listened, the whole meeting and the message seemed to be for me."

When the time came for those who wanted to accept Jesus Christ as Saviour to go forward, Robina said to her husband, "I'm going forward. Will you come?"

"No," he replied. "If you go, you go on your own."

But then, he says, he remembers "hanging on to the seat just as tightly as I possibly could, and then I don't remember anything else other than being down there with her, with my arms around her weeping."

And Billy Graham, as he usually does, suggested that those who had come forward should go home to pray and thank God for what had happened. He also suggested that they should start reading the Bible and tell someone what they had done.

LES DENNISON
Former Communist

Revelation 3:20

Dennison's background in the coal mines and car factories led him in the 1930s to Communism, and he gained a reputation for being one of the most obstructive organizers. At home, he was violent and the family was on the point of breaking up. Then a shop steward at work, a Christian, lost his temper with Les and told him that all his talk of uniting the workers was useless if he couldn't unite his own family.

Les knew the charge was well founded, and agreed to meet a couple of his mate's Christian friends. He started thinking about absolute standards of morality and integrity, and questioned his assumption that the individual was the victim of his environment.

Les went to church, and afterwards allowed the minister to pray with him. The vicar quoted Revelation 3:20, where Jesus says, "Here I am! I stand at the door and knock," and Les was filled with a sense of the evil in him. He prayed briefly for God's help, and as the vicar continued to pray Les felt inward release. As he left the church he knew a peace he had never known before.

VINCE DiMAGGIO
American baseball player

Sitting at home

Every night Vince DiMaggio would be found checking the baseball scores in the newspaper. This night was no exception. When his wife, Madeline, asked him if he minded her having the television on, he did not object, although when he found it was a Billy Graham programme he suggested trying a different channel. Religious programmes were not the sort of thing he wanted to hear. "Isn't these anything else on?" he asked.

But Madeline wanted that particular programme, so Vince put up with it. He was not at all interested, but at the end of the broadcast Madeline seemed pleased that she had watched it.

Billy Graham was on the next evening as well, and the evening after that. Each time, Madeline put the television on and Vince buried himself in his newspaper – but despite himself he was now beginning to listen to some of what the evangelist was saying. On the second night some of Billy's message was getting through despite his newspaper; on the third night the newspaper was only a pretence, a shield behind which he was secretly listening to every word of the evangelistic programme. He did not want to let his wife know he was listening.

At the end of the third night's sermon, Vince dropped his paper and looked at the screen as Billy turned to the camera and pointed, urging viewers in bars or in their own homes home to accept Jesus. He seemed to be staring straight at Vince.

Without knowing what he was doing, Vince dropped out of his chair and on to his knees. How it happened he could not afterwards recall, but he remembered that he was crying. Right then and there, in his own home, he accepted Jesus as his Lord.

SIR WILLIAM DOBBIE   *Burden lifted*
British Army General, famed for his defence of Malta in World War II

The young William Dobbie came to trust Jesus Christ as his Saviour when he was a pupil at Charterhouse School.

Even as a boy, he felt the burden of sin, and felt it a very great burden. One Sunday evening, he suddenly realized that Christ had died in order to put away William Dobbie's sins and to blot them out. That evening, William knew that God, for Christ's sake, forgave his sins.

Much later in his life, the soldier considered that evening without any question as a real and final transaction. God had dealt with all his sins, including those he had committed since that time. He knew he had continued to fall into sin many, many times, but they had all been dealt with by Christ's death. He took comfort from the fact that it was not anything which he had done but rather what Christ had done, that formed the basis for his forgiveness.

"I would not dream of facing life in the army or out of it," he would say, "without Christ. I do not know how people can go on trying to live without Him."

JOHN DODD *Prison experiences*
Founder of the Langley House Trust
working with discharged prisoners

John Dodd managed to survive imprisonment at the hands of the Japanese in World War II, but he was battered both physically and emotionally by the experience. Back home, when he reluctantly accompanied his mother to a Methodist service, he heard some words from the prophecy of Joel – "I will restore to you the years that the locust hath eaten" – which he thought were an apt description of the war years.

Then, on the wireless, he heard a talk by the Bishop of Singapore, who like himself had been a prisoner in Changi. John was impressed by the Bishop's total lack of bitterness, and his deepened faith.

He kept meeting Christians, and eventually he came to see that there was a God of love and a meaning to life. Although he does not remember what day it was, there came a time when he gave his life to God. Later he likened this to a Liverpool football fan becoming an Everton supporter.

He joined the local Methodist church and, after some time, the minister suggested he take up prison visiting. When he began visiting prisoners in Parkhurst Prison, he was not just sorry for them, but his own wartime experiences gave him a profound sympathy for them.

FYODOR DOSTOEVSKY   *In a Russian prison camp*
Russian novelist

Dostoevsky had believed that Christ was both God and man for some time, but he had thought of Him mainly as a transformer of society. But in a Russian prison camp he came to think of Him in a more personal and intimate way. As he faced what seemed like a certain death he found that Christ Himself encouraged him. His faith in Christ could no longer be shaken.

KITRINA DOUGLAS   *At the age of seven*
British professional golfer

Kitrina grew up in a Christian family and recalls going to church one day with her dad as a seven-year-old. During the service the preacher asked people to put up their hands if they wanted to give their lives to Jesus Christ. Kitrina first checked with her dad that it was all right to do this and then went ahead and put up her hand. From that night Kitrina marks the start of her Christian life.

However, Kitrina would be the first person to admit that she did not experience a great deal of growth in the early stages of her Christian life. But more recently, when a British newspaper reporter remarked that she behaved as if she wanted to be a missionary, she was happy to reply that she was already a missionary, in her golfing world.

BOB DYLAN   *"A vision and a feeling"*
Singer

Dylan's 1979 album *Slow Train Coming* splashed his conversion story on the front pages of newspapers across the world. When questioned about this experience, Dylan said that it happened the year before in a room which, he maintained, actually moved as he had "a vision and a feeling".

Dylan recalls that "There was a presence in the room that couldn't have been anybody but Jesus." Dylan points out that many people think that Christian conversion experiences come in the main to those who are down-and-outs in their souls. Dylan found the opposite to be true. He was doing fine and was not dissatisfied with life.

Because a friend whom Dylan respected had mentioned Jesus to him Dylan went along to a Christian community which was full of born-again believers. As a result of this he could accept the reality of Christ in his mind. Later, at his home, Dylan was asked if he wanted Christ in his life, and that day he prayed and received Christ as his Lord. Speaking about this, Dylan says, "I truly had a born-again experience."

JONATHAN EDWARDS
American philosopher and revival preacher

Swallowed up in God

Edwards was converted when he was nearly 18. His conversion story ranks with those of people like Augustine and Pascal, whose experience of the risen Christ is beyond words. Here is Edwards' own stumbling attempt to express the inexpressible:

> A calm, sweet Abstraction of the Soul from all Concerns of this World; and a kind of Vision, or fix'd Ideas and Imaginations, of being alone in the Mountains, or some solitary Wilderness, far from all Mankind; sweetly conversing with Christ, and wrapt and swallowed up in God. The Sense I had of divine Things would often of a sudden as it were, kindle up a sweet burning in my Heart; an ardour of my Soul, that I know not how to express.

At about this time Edwards read 1 Timothy 1:17, "Now to the King eternal, immortal, invisible, the only God, be honour and glory for ever and ever. Amen." After he had read this scripture he had another experience of Christ:

> There came into my soul, and was as it were diffused through it, a sense of the glory of the Divine Being; a new sense, quite

81

different from anything I had experienced before. From about that time I began to have a new kind of apprehension and idea of Christ, and the work of redemption, and the glorious way of salvation by him.

EDWIN
7th-century king of Northumbria

A king's vision, seen in exile

King Ethelfrid of Northumbria was persecuting Edwin, a Northumbrian nobleman. So Edwin fled to Redwald, King of East Anglia, to live under his protection. Ethelfrid tried to bribe Redwald into giving Edwin up and threatened to attack him if he would not. Redwald agreed that he would either kill Edwin or give him up to Ethelfrid. A friend of Edwin heard about this plan and warned him, suggesting that he should escape with him. Edwin refused to escape, and stayed in Redwald's palace, a very frightened man.

One night Edwin encountered a stranger, but Edwin was not startled. The stranger came up to him, put his right hand on his head and asked him why he was so worried. Edwin asked the stranger why he was out so late at night. The stranger replied that he knew all about Edwin's plight and told him to stop worrying. Then he asked Edwin what kind of reward he would give a person if Redwald could be persuaded not to kill him nor hand him over to Ethelfrid. Edwin said he would give the largest reward he was able to give if this happened.

Then the stranger asked what kind of reward Edwin would give if he defeated his enemies and became a powerful king. Edwin said that he would give a fitting reward if this happened.

Then the stranger asked what kind of reward Edwin would give if in addition to all this Edwin received better advice for his salvation and his life than he had ever been given in the past. Edwin promised that he would follow the teachings of any person who delivered him from his present troubles and made him king.

The stranger told Edwin to remember his promise to him

when these things did take place, and he then vanished from sight.

As Edwin was pondering this vision his friend came and told him that Redwald had had a change of heart and was not going to kill him or give him over to Ethelfrid. This happened. Redwald even attacked and killed Ethelfrid.

Edwin became king but did not embrace the Christian faith as he had promised to. Bishop Paulinus came up to Edwin and put his right hand on his head and reminded him to keep his promise. Edwin trembled from head to toe. He agreed that he and his advisers would all consecrate themselves to Christ. He also agreed that Paulinus should destroy the temples of the idols which the people were worshipping.

Edwin was baptized at York on 12th April 627, the day before Easter, in the church of St Peter the Apostle. Edwin replaced this wooden church with a church built of stone on the site of the modern York Minster.

JOHN ELIAS   *On the way to Pwllheli*
19th-century Welsh preacher

The Lord was pleased to send stronger illuminations to my mind respecting doctrines of the Gospel, and the method of grace in saving sinners. One day – I remember it well, in a certain place on the way to Pwllheli – the words "the ministry of reconciliation", etc. (2 Corinthians 5:18–19) came to my mind with some light which was quite strange to me. My soul had such a feast in the words, that "God was in Christ reconciling the world unto himself, not imputing their trespasses unto them"! I saw that the way to accomplish this was by imputing our sins to Christ, and imputing his righteousness unto us (verse 21). The doctrine of imputation has been, since that time, of infinite importance in my estimation. I felt from the pleasure I experienced then in that word, that I could preach it to my countrymen everywhere.

Life and Letters, John Elias, Banner of Truth, 1973, pp. 17–18

JIM ELLIOT
About six years old

**Missionary to the Auca Indians
in Ecuador, and modern martyr**

The Elliot family did not have much of a chance to escape Christianity. From the age of six weeks they went to church with their parents. Jim's father, Fred Elliot, read the Bible to his children every day. He always tried to pray with them and not at them or for them. One by one each of the Elliot children asked the Lord Jesus Christ to be his or her own personal Friend and Saviour.

On one occasion when the family had just returned from going to church, and when Jim was only about six, he said to his mother, "Now, mama, the Lord Jesus can come whenever He wants. He could take our whole family, because I'm saved now, and Janie is too young to know about Him yet."

After this Jim told his friends that he had Jesus as his special Friend who had forgiven him all his sins. He did this as he swung to and fro on the swing in the family's garden.

CHARLOTTE ELLIOTT
"Just as you are"

19th-century hymn-writer

While staying in Clapham in 1822, Dr Caesar Malan, of Geneva, asked the daughter of the house if she was a Christian. The young lady, Charlotte Elliott, loved music and drawing, but had no time for religion and disliked the visitor's question. When Dr Malan saw this, he told her he would pray that she would give her heart to Christ and become a useful worker for Him. Eventually, his prayers were answered, for Charlotte asked him how she could find Christ.

"Come to Him just as you are," he answered.

She did so, and went on to write about 150 hymns, including the famous lines:

> Just as I am, without one plea
> But that thy blood was shed for me,

And that thou bidst me come to thee,
O Lamb of God, I come.

"For those in sickness and sorrow," says Julian's *Dictionary of Hymnology*, "she has sung as few others have done."

ETHIOPIAN EUNUCH
1st-century royal treasurer
Scriptures explained

Now an angel of the Lord said to Philip, "Go south to the road – the desert road – that goes down from Jerusalem to Gaza." So he started out, and on his way he met an Ethiopian eunuch, an important official in charge of all the treasury of Candace, queen of the Ethiopians. This man had gone to Jerusalem to worship, and on his way home was sitting in his chariot reading the book of Isaiah the prophet. The Spirit told Philip, "Go to that chariot and stay near it."

Then Philip ran up to the chariot and heard the man reading Isaiah the prophet. "Do you understand what you are reading?" Philip asked.

"How can I," he said, "unless someone explains it to me?" So he invited Philip to come up and sit with him.

The eunuch was reading this passage of Scripture:

"He was led like a sheep to the slaughter,
and as a lamb before the shearer is silent,
so he did not open his mouth.
In his humiliation he was deprived of justice.
Who can speak of his descendants?
For his life was taken from the earth."

The eunuch asked Philip, "Tell me, please, who is the prophet talking about, himself or someone else?" Then Philip began with that very passage of Scripture and told him the good news about Jesus.

As they travelled along the road, they came to some water and the eunuch said, "Look, here is water. Why shouldn't I be baptised?" And he ordered the chariot to stop. Then both

Philip and the eunuch went down into the water and Philip baptised him. When they came up out of the water, the Spirit of the Lord suddenly took Philip away, and the eunuch did not see him again, but went on his way rejoicing. Philip, however, appeared at Azotus and travelled about, preaching the gospel in all the towns until he reached Caesarea.

Acts 8:26–40

JUSTIN FASHANU   *Five hours of questions*
Footballer

Fashanu became a Christian on 22nd May 1982. This was how it happened.

He had an accident with his sponsored Toyota car and took it in to be repaired. As he went to collect the repaired car Fashanu was a little taken aback to be asked by the man in the garage, Terry Carpenter, "Are you happy?" Fashanu knew that he was far from being happy.

For the next five hours Fashanu and Carpenter talked and talked about Christianity. Fashanu was firing the questions and Carpenter was doing his best to provide the answers. In fact Carpenter answered Fashanu's questions so helpfully that the footballer came to see that Carpenter had something that he wanted.

In the car showroom Fashanu got down on his knees and accepted the Lord Jesus Christ into his life.

CHARLES FINNEY   *"The very breath of God"*
19th-century American evangelist

The spiritual experiences which render Finney's name an outstanding one in Revival annals began soon after he entered the office of Mr Benjamin Wright, at Adams, N.Y., in 1818, when, as he assures us in his *Memoirs*:

"I was almost as ignorant of religion as a heathen. I had been brought up mostly in the woods. I had very little regard to the Sabbath, and had no definite knowledge of religious truth."

In the course of his legal studies, however, he found that sundry authors made frequent reference to the Mosaic Law and therefore, for professional reasons alone, he purchased a Bible. He also came into contact with a number of professing Christians, but they were dead and worldly, and he pointed out to them, in frigid terms, that their prayers were never answered: "You have prayed enough since I have attended these meetings to have prayed the devil out of town, if there were any virtue in your prayers. But here you are, praying and complaining still." On further reading the Bible, however, it struck Finney that the reason why their prayers were not answered was simply because they did not comply with the revealed conditions upon which God had promised to answer prayer. The thought, at any rate, relieved his doubts; yet he was brought face to face with the question, whether he would yield his whole being to Christ or pursue a career of worldly emulation and personal aggrandisement.

While hesitating thus between ambition and Christianity, he seemed to hear a voice speak from heaven to his soul, and he resolved to seek the Lord, if haply he might find Him. Going out into the woods to pray, he found a sanctuary between some fallen trees; but he realised that he was more anxious lest some passer-by should notice him than he was to have his sins forgiven and become a child of the Kingdom. Then, while he was broken and abased before God, the Spirit impressed upon his mind the words from the Book of Jeremiah: "Then shall ye find Me, when ye shall seek for Me with all your heart" [Jeremiah 29:13]. Thus he sought, and thus he found. On the same evening, as he went to his room "it seemed as if I met the Lord Jesus Christ face to face. It did not occur to me then, nor did it for some time afterwards, that it was wholly a mental state. It seemed to me a reality that He stood before me, and I fell down and poured out my soul to Him."

So he continued in communion and prayer, when – again to give his own words: "Without any expectation of it, without ever having the thought in my mind that there was such a thing for me, without any recollection that I had ever heard the thing mentioned by any person in the world, the Holy Spirit descended upon me in a manner that seemed to go through me, body and soul ... It seemed like the very breath of God. I wept aloud with joy and love."

The news of his conversion was received with incredulity, so bitter had he been against the church-members. "If religion is true," scoffers had said, "why don't you convert Finney? If you can do that, we will believe in religion." Even the minister, with whom he had often spoken, refused to credit the story. But, in the evening, there was a general movement towards the Presbyterian church. The place was thronged with an expectant congregation; and Finney, without waiting for a formal opening, related, with simplicity and directness, his experience of the Lord's dealing with him. That meeting was the beginning of a Revival which changed the character of the district.

Quoted in *Finney's Life and Lectures*, edited by William Henry Harding, Oliphants, 1943, pp. 1–3

JOHN FLETCHER
18th-century vicar of Madeley, England

"My heart was as hard as flint"

The 12th of January 1755, I received the Sacrament, though my heart was as hard as flint. The following day, I felt the tyranny of sin more than ever, and an uncommon coldness in all religious duties. I felt the burden of my corruptions heavier than ever; there was no rest in my flesh. I called upon the Lord, but with such heaviness as made me fear it was lost labour. The more I prayed for victory over sin, the more I was conquered. Many a time did I take up the Bible to seek comfort, but not being able to read, I shut it again. The thoughts which engrossed my mind, were generally these. I am undone. I have wandered from God more than ever. – I have trampled under foot the frequent convictions which God was pleased to work in my heart. Instead of going straight to Christ, I have wasted my time in fighting against sin with the dim light of my reason, and the mere use of the means of grace; as if the means would do me good without the blessing and power of God. I fear my knowledge of Christ is only speculative, and does not reach my heart. I *never had faith*; and without faith it is impossible to please God. Therefore, all my thoughts, words, and works, however specious before men, are utterly sinful before God. And if I am not washed and renewed before I go hence, I am lost to all eternity.

When I saw all my endeavours availed nothing toward conquering sin, I almost gave up all hope, and resolved to sin on, and go to Hell ... I would here observe that anger in particular, seemed to be one of the sins I could never overcome. – So I went on sinning and repenting, and sinning again; but still calling on God's Mercy through Christ.

I was now beat out of all my strongholds. I felt my helplessness, and lay at the feet of Christ. I cried, though *coldly*, yet I believe *sincerely*, "Save me, Lord, as a brand snatched out of the fire; give me justifying faith in thy blood; cleanse me from my sins; for the devil will surely reign over me, until thou shalt take me into thy hand. I shall only be an instrument in his hand to work wickedness, until thou shalt stretch forth thine almighty arm, and save thy lost creature by free unmerited grace."...

On Sunday the 19th, in the evening, I heard an excellent sermon on these words, – "Being justified by faith, we have peace with God, through our Lord Jesus Christ." I heard it attentively, but my heart was not moved in the least; I was only still more convinced, that I was an unbeliever, that I was not justified by faith, and that till I was, I should never have peace with God ...

I begged of God, the following day, to shew me the wickedness of my heart, and to fit me for his pardoning mercy: I besought him to increase my convictions, for I was afraid, I did not *mourn* enough for my sins. But I found relief in Mr Wesley's Journal, where I learned that we should not build on what we feel; but go to Christ, with all our sins and all our hardness of heart ...

Thursday, my Fast-Day, Satan beset me hard: I sinned, and grievously too. And now I almost gave up all hope. I mourned deeply, but with an heart as hard as ever. I was on the brink of despair, and continued nevertheless to fall into sin, as often as I had temptation. But I must observe that all this while, though I had a clear sense of my wickedness, and of what I deserved; and though I often thought that hell would be my portion, yet I never was much afraid of it. Whether this was owing to a secret hope lodged in my mind, or to hardness of heart, I know not; but I was continually crying out, "What stupidity! I see myself hanging as by a thread over Hell! and yet I am not afraid – but sin on! O what is man without the grace of God! a very devil in wickedness, though inferior to him in experience and power." In the evening, I went to a friend, and told him something of my present state; he endeavoured to administer comfort, but it did not suit my case: There is no Peace to a sinner, unless it come from above. When we parted, he gave me some advice which suited my condition better. "God (said he) is merciful; God loves you; and if he deny you any thing, it is for your good; you deserve nothing at his hands, wait then patiently for him, and *never* give up your *hope*." I went home resolved to follow his advice, though I should stay till death ...

I then went to bed, commending myself to God with rather more hope and peace than I had felt for some time. But Satan waked, while I slept. I dreamed I had committed grievous and abominable sins; I awoke amazed and confounded, and rising, with a detestation of the corruption of my senses and imagination, I fell upon my knees, and prayed with more faith and less wanderings than usual; and afterward went about my business with an uncommon cheerfulness. It was not long before I was tempted by my besetting sin, but found myself a new creature. My soul was not even ruffled ... The more I prayed, the more I saw it was real. For though sin stirred all the day long, I always overcame it in the Name of the Lord ...

I continued calling upon the Lord for an increase of faith; for still I felt some fear of being in a delusion: And having continued my supplication till near one in the morning, I then opened my Bible on these words, Psalm 55:22: "Cast thy burden on the Lord, and he shall sustain thee; he will not suffer the righteous to be moved." Filled with joy, I fell again on my knees to beg of God, that I might always cast my burden upon him. I took up my Bible again, and opened it on these words, Deut. 31: "I will be with thee; I will not fail thee, neither forsake thee; fear not neither be dismayed." My hope was now greatly increased, and I thought I saw myself conqueror over sin, hell, and all manner of affliction.

With this comfortable promise I shut up my Bible, being now perfectly satisfied. As I shut it, I cast my eye on that word, "Whatsoever you shall ask in my name, I will do it." So having asked grace of God to serve him till death, I went cheerfully to take my rest.

The Life of the Rev. John William de la Flechere, Joseph Benson, Methodist Conference-Office, 1805, pp. 16–21

TERRY FONTANE   *Road accident*
American pop singer

A road accident stopped Terry Fontane in his tracks. One moment he was hurtling along in his sports car; the next (conscious) moment he was in a hospital bed, unable to see or walk or sit up.

He'd been brought up in a thoroughly Christian home, his parents living very simply in order to run a rescue mission for down-and-outs. Terry resented it all, and was pleased when his singing career took off and led him to Beverly Hills. Soon he had a wife and a daughter and plenty of money – and that sports car.

He was only angry when a hospital chaplain tried to talk to him; but his tether broke when, just at the time his sight was beginning to return, he had a visit from his wife who announced that she had just become a Christian and was convinced that God answered prayer "just like your mum and dad have always said". Terry just collapsed in his wife's embrace, and prayed to God to forgive him for his years of rebellion.

It was three months before Terry was allowed out of hospital, and then he refused to take up his old career. His singing voice he put at God's disposal, to be used only for giving his testimony and in sacred concerts.

GEORGE FOX *Inner light*
Founder of the Society of Friends (the Quakers)

When Fox was about twenty years old he knew spiritual longings which he could not explain – he felt in his life a sense of incompleteness, as if a part of his nature had not come to its true home. "I went to many a priest to look for comfort, but found no comfort from them." His position may be compared with that of a man born blind who knows much, not about light, but about optics, the science of light. Such a one might have mathematical knowledge of his subject, might by means of models know how the rays of light behave in passing through a lens or prism, might understand the mechanism of optical instruments and even suggest improvements in them – such a thing is conceivable – and yet about *light itself* he would know nothing. To all his enquiries no answer could be given even by those who themselves had knowledge. But if by some means he is enabled to see, he has an experience of *his own* which all his learning could not in itself give him. He need not undervalue his previous knowledge in view of the great experience into which he has come, but for the first time he knows what lies at the back of it and what it all means. He has personal assurance which he has not acquired by demonstration of others and which he cannot demonstrate to another. In like manner, Fox had, in a sense, not been ignorant of God; he had reached after Him, studied the Bible, lived righteously; but now there came into his life his own personal apprehension of God satisfying his soul's need. This is knowledge toward which one may help another by reasoning or counsel and, above all, by the attraction of love, but like all knowledge of the deep things of life it cannot be forced on anyone.

About the beginning of the year 1646, as I was going to Coventry, and approaching toward the gate, a consideration arose in me, how it was said that "all Christians are believers, both Protestants and Papists;" and the Lord opened to me that, if all were believers, then they were all born of God, and passed from death to life, and that none were true believers but such; and though others said they were believers, yet they were not. At another time, as I was walking in a field on a first-day morning, the Lord opened unto me, "that being bred at Oxford or Cambridge was not enough to fit and qualify men to be ministers of Christ;" and I wondered at it, because it was the common belief of people. But I saw it clearly as the Lord opened it to me ...

One day when I had been walking solitarily abroad, and was come home, I was wrapped up in the love of God, so that I could not but admire the greatness of his love. While I was in that condition, it was opened unto me by the eternal light and power, and I saw clearly therein, "that all was done, and to be done, in and by Christ; and how he conquers and destroys this tempter, the Devil, and all his works, and is above him; and that all these troubles were good for me, and temptations for the trial of my faith, which Christ had given me." The Lord opened me, that I saw through all these troubles and temptations; my living faith was raised, that I saw all was done by Christ, the life, and my belief was in him.

The Personality of George Fox, A. Neave Brayshaw, Allenson, 1933, pp 13–14; *Journal of George Fox*, 7th ed., Cash and others, 1852, vol. I, pp. 50–57

"Let yourself go" was the advice James Fox had from some of his friends – but he wasn't so sure. In fact, he felt that this way led to a horrible black abyss which would destroy him.

Searching for a positive alternative, he recalled from his public-school chapel days the verse, "Come unto me, all ye who labour and are heavy-laden, and I will give you rest" (Matthew 11:28). He tried living a decent life, going to Communion on Sundays, but it was boring. He found no-one who could help him. But he felt like the Prodigal Son in the parable, who came to his senses and went home, and when he was still some distance from his home his father came running to meet him.

In Fox's case, his heavenly Father came to him in the following way. While performing in a play in Blackpool, he was staying in a hotel, where he got talking to a man he met at the breakfast table. When Fox asked the man what he was doing in Blackpool, the reply was, "Spending a day with the Lord." Fox felt that this man had been sent by God to help him. He told this total stranger about the emptiness of his religious search, and in return the man talked in terms that were quite new to Fox about God's plan of salvation – which he drew on a serviette!

As Fox himself later described it: "To believe was not hard; the facts were offered to me in honest and simple truths by eye-witnesses that compelled trust. But to turn was harder. There was the risk of losing something, of surrendering my legitimate control over my own life, of yielding up my liberty. There was the challenge to change my way of life, my attitude to right and wrong.

"What about my money? Who would I be meant to marry? Would I have to become a missionary? These sorts of questions, which in all honesty I had to be willing to have answered by the sovereign choice of God Himself, were harder.

"But what my eyes fell upon, as I reflected on the literature Bernie had left me, was this verse: 'But God shows His love

for us in that while we were yet sinners, Christ died for us.'
Didn't I dare to risk losing something of this life? Did this loss
compare with Jesus, who gave up all, His whole life, that I
might be given life? Couldn't I trust Him with all my future?
If not, who could I trust?

"That night I knelt down beside my hotel bed in simple
response."

FRANCIS OF ASSISI   *God's fool*
13th-century founder of the Franciscan friars

Francis ... underwent a reversal of a certain psychological
kind; which was really like the reversal of a complete som-
ersault, in that by coming full circle it came back, or apparently came back, to the same normal posture. It is necessary
to use the grotesque simile of an acrobatic antic, because
there is hardly any other figure that will make the fact clear.
But in the inward sense it was a profound spiritual revolution. The man who went into the cave was not the man who
came out again; in that sense he was almost as different as if
he were dead, as if he were a ghost or a blessed spirit. And the
effects of this on his attitude towards the actual world were
really as extravagant as any parallel can make them. He
looked at the world as differently from other men as if he had
come out of that dark hole walking on his hands ...

It may be suspected that in that black cell or cave Francis
passed the blackest hours of his life. By nature he was the sort
of man who has that vanity which is the opposite of pride;
that vanity which is very near to humility ... He had made a
fool of himself. Any man who has been young, who has ridden
horses or thought himself ready for a fight, who has fancied
himself as a troubadour and accepted the conventions of
comradeship, will appreciate the ponderous and crushing
weight of that simple phrase. The conversion of St Francis,
like that of St Paul, involved his being in some sense flung
suddenly from a horse; but in a sense it was an even worse
fall; for it was a war-horse. Anyhow, there was not a rag of

him left that was not ridiculous. Everybody knew that at the best he had made a fool of himself ...

When Francis came forth from his cave of vision, he was wearing the same word "fool" as a feather in his cap; as a crest or even a crown. He would go on being a fool: he would become more and more of a fool; he would be the court fool of the King of Paradise.

St. Francis of Assisi, G. K. Chesterton, Hodder & Stoughton, 1923, pp. 83–87

JOHN FRENCH
British actor
Hatred evaporated

John French's fiancée had been converted at Billy Graham's Harringay crusade, and as she spent time reading her Bible and developing a new, confident personality John recognized that they were drifting apart. She was to play the lead role in a Billy Graham film; John was becoming more hostile, and still his fiancée remained patient and serene.

John convinced himself that he was losing his fiancée because the Billy Graham organization were taking her away from him; he told the press as much, and tried to humiliate Billy Graham himself in an angry encounter. But the evangelist was not to be humiliated, and John found himself asking for help, despite himself. He knew his life was empty, and he felt sorry for himself. He was beginning to feel a great urge to encounter God for himself.

Billy Graham told him that Jesus had died to save everyone, including John French. John's hatred was evaporating, his struggle abandoned. He went home to read John's Gospel and found that he could, for the first time, understand it.

"It was a miracle all right. It completely changed my life, my outlook, my thoughts, my vision, my soul and my heart. I felt as if the latter was being impregnated with the Spirit of God – the Holy Spirit. I was changing and becoming a new person. I was re-born, and it was reality!"

ELIZABETH FRY
19th-century champion
of British prison reform

*Through William
Savery's preaching*

William Savery had come from America to this country on a visit of gospel love, in the course of which he attended the usual Meeting at Norwich on first day, the 4th of second month, 1798.

His preaching was very impressive: he was through the power of the Holy Spirit, qualified, in no common degree, for the office of an ambassador for Christ. In his own published journal is this reference to the above-mentioned visit to Norwich.

> Very few middle-aged or young persons who had a consistent appearance in their dress; indeed, I thought it the gayest Meeting of Friends I ever sat in, and was grieved to see it. Several of the younger branches, though they were enabled through divine grace to see what the Truth leads to, yet it is uncertain whether, with all the alluring things of this world around them, they will choose the simple, safe path of self-denial.

Elizabeth's sister, Richenda, thus describes this eventful day:

> Betsy was generally rather restless at Meeting; and on this day, I remember her very smart boots were a great amusement to me; they were purple, laced with scarlet.
>
> At last William Savery began to preach. His voice and manner were arresting, and we all liked the sound; her attention became fixed: at last I saw her begin to weep, and she became a good deal agitated. She wept most of the way home. The next morning, William Savery came to breakfast, prophesying of the high and important calling Betsy would be led into. What she went through in her own mind, I cannot say, but the results were most powerful, and most evident. From that day her love of pleasure and of the world seemed gone.

How deep the impression, made upon the mind of Elizabeth, her own journal portrays.

> I wish the state of enthusiasm I am in may last, for to-day I have felt *that there is a God;* I have been devotional, and my mind has

97

been led away from the follies that it is mostly wrapt up in. We had much serious conversation; in short, what he said and what I felt, was like a refreshing shower falling upon earth, and had been dried up for ages. It has not made me unhappy: I have felt ever since humble. I have longed for virtue. I hope to be truly virtuous; to let sophistry fly from my mind; not to be enthusiastic and foolish; but only to be so far religious as will lead to virtue. There seems nothing so little understood as religion.

"What little religion I have felt has been owing to my giving way quietly and humbly to my feelings; but the more I reason upon it, the more I get into a labyrinth of uncertainty, and my mind is so much inclined to both scepticism and enthusiasm, that if I argue and doubt, I shall be a total sceptic; if, on the contrary, I give way to my feelings, and as it were, wait for religion, I may be led away.

March 17th.
May I never forget the impression William Savery has made on my mind! as much as I can say is, I thank God for having sent at least a glimmering of light, through him, into my heart, which I hope with care, and keeping it from the many draughts and winds of this life, may not be blown out, but become a large brilliant flame, that will direct me to that haven, where will be joy without sorrow, and all will be comfort.

May I never lose the little religion I now have; but if I cannot feel religion and devotion, I must not despair, for I am truly warm and earnest in the cause, it will come one day. I fear and tremble for myself, but I must humbly look to the Author of all that is good and great, and, I may say, humbly pray, that He will take me as a sheep strayed from His flock, and once more let me enter the fold of His glory. I feel there is a God and Immortality; happy, happy thought! May it never leave me, and if it should, may I remember I have *felt* that there is a God and Immortality.

Thirty years afterwards, in 1828, she thus reviews this critical period of life.

I felt the vanity and folly of what are called the pleasures of this life, of which the tendency is not to satisfy, but eventually to enervate and injure the heart and mind; those only are real pleasures which are of an innocent nature, and used as recreations, subjected to the cross of Christ. I was, in my judgment, much confirmed in the infinite importance of religion, as the only real stay, guide, help, and comfort in this life, and the only means of our having a hope of partaking of a better.

98

Can any one doubt, that it was His Spirit which manifested to me the evil in my own heart, as well as that which I perceived around me? leading me to abhor it, and to hunger and thirst after Himself, and His righteousness, and that salvation which cometh by Christ.

MITSUO FUCHIDA
Japanese Presbyterian minister and former World War II pilot

"The Holy Spirit alone made it plain"

Mitsuo Fuchida was once a Japanese airman, who led the raid on Pearl Harbour on 7th December, 1941. His spiritual pilgrimage led him through Shintoism, Buddhism and Emperor Worship to Christianity.

On a journey to Tokyo in 1949 to meet General Mac-Arthur, he was given a tract entitled, *I Was A Prisoner of Japan*. It told the story of Jacob de Shazer, an American who had been captured in special missions behind the Japanese lines. In prison he had been given a Bible, and through reading it had come to know Jesus Christ as his own Master and Lord. After the war he had returned to Japan as a missionary to the people whom he had once fought and hated.

The testimony of this tract had a profound effect on ex-Commander Fuchida and he began to read the Bible carefully himself.

"One month after the tract was given to me I read in Luke's Gospel the words, 'Father, forgive them for they know not what they do', and it came home to me just what the Lord Jesus Christ had done for me. No one helped me to understand it; the Holy Spirit alone made it plain."

Following his conversion he dedicated the remainder of his life to the service of Jesus Christ, and was eventually ordained to the Presbyterian ministry, visiting towns and villages telling the people the Gospel of Christ.

CHARLES E. FULLER
America's most popular revivalist in the 1930s and 1940s

In the shade of a eucalyptus tree

Charles Fuller grew up in a Christian family in which reading the Bible was part of their daily life. However, Charles did not show any visible sign of benefiting spiritually from any of this for the first 29 years of his life.

He attended the local Presbyterian church in Placentia, where he worked as a manager of the growers' cooperative packing plant. In July 1916 his interest was aroused by the announcement that the former boxer and wrestler, Paul Rader, was to preach in the Church of the Open Door in Los Angeles. As Charles had played American football for Placentia he decided to drive to Los Angeles to hear what this former athlete had to say.

The more Paul Rader spoke about Jesus Christ being the Saviour of the world, the more uncomfortable Charles became. He ended up by leaning forward onto the seat in front of him, and he began to tremble because he was so convicted about his sinful ways. However, he did not have the courage to go to the front of the church when Rader made his appeal to those who wanted to say in public that they were prepared to follow Christ. Instead Charles got into his car and drove to Franklin Park in Hollywood. There, in the shade of a eucalyptus tree, he asked Christ to come into his life.

During the 1940s Charles Fuller broadcast the "Old Fashioned Revival Hour", which became one of the most popular radio programmes in the United States.

PRINCESS CATHERINE GALITZINE
Russian Princess

In an American chapel in Russia

Princess Lieven was visited by Princess Catherine Galitzine. They went by sleigh to a Communion service at a Greek

Orthodox Church. Princess Galitzine found the service very moving, and regretted that she had to wait until the next service before she could have these wonderful inner feelings again.

She thought about this as she went home to her palace with her friend Princess Lieven. There she met Lord Radstock, an English evangelist, and the Princess told him all about the delight she had found in the Communion service. Lord Radstock asked the two princesses if they would like to have this experience with them all the time. He then explained how this could happen if they had Jesus Christ as their own personal Saviour and Friend. Later Princess Galitzine heard Lord Radstock preach in the American Chapel. She spoke to him after the service and in that chapel knelt down with Lord Radstock and gave her life to Jesus Christ.

MARTIN GALIWANGO
Ugandan

Search for satisfaction

From the age of 13, Martin knew there was something missing in his life.

He thought at first that his confirmation might fill the gap, but he found joy in that for only a day.

Then he thought getting a paid job might satisfy him, but he got miserable when his money ran out.

Then he got married, but found that neither wife nor children gave him what he wanted.

He defrauded his employers and made himself rich, and on the strength of that he built himself a house and drank a lot. But still he had not found peace.

In the end he went to a mission at his church and heard the preacher say that because of man's fallen nature he would never derive satisfaction from such things, but only from Jesus. "Yes, Lord, I come!" responded Martin. He did indeed experience peace then; and he told his wife and friends and former employers what had happened. His wife became a Christian, and his employers declined to prosecute, giving him time to make restitution as and when he could.

HENRIETTA GANT   *Vision of welcome*
Black American from Louisiana slave stock

The Federal Writers' Project archives include a long interview with Henrietta Gant, who was over 60 when she was interviewed in 1939.

She had been a Christian for 22 years. She told the Project interviewer how she had gone off by herself, while her husband was out in the fields cutting sugar cane, and she had just talked to God all day for about three weeks. She had wanted Him to talk with her just like the interviewer was talking to her, she said. But her experience was of God coming to her in a gold chariot from the clouds and welcoming her home. She was frightened, and was not sure she was a Christian, so she asked for a sign; she asked that the sun would shout three times. The sun came out from behind the clouds and, she says, shouted to her three times, bowed, and went back behind the clouds.

Then one night Henrietta got up at midnight and prayed to God to convert her. By four o'clock the Spirit had come to her and she was ready to be baptized. She insisted that in order to get the Spirit you had to pray – she was praying at home, and when the Spirit came she shouted out and woke her neighbours.

She had a vision of a white house on a hill, with the Lord standing at the open door. He took her in and laid her on an operating table. Then He took her heart out, scraped it and put it back. The Father, the Son and the Mother were there, all dressed in white, and the Mother asked Henrietta why she had come. She replied that she had come to work, and the Mother took her to another room which was full of little children all dressed in white and wearing crowns. Henrietta took this to be a sign that she was teach in the Sunday

Her philosophy was: if you trust the Lord for something, you should trust Him for everything. If you don't, you don't have faith.

COLONEL JAMES GARDINER
19th-century Colonel in the
British Army

Instantaneous
and complete

A sudden and complete transformation took place in the life of Colonel Gardiner when he was in the prime of manhood, in the full flush of health, and in the active pursuit of an adulterous amour. It was also instantaneous and complete; there was no protracted conflict; no mastering darling sins one day to fall a victim to them the next; but all the principles, motives, affections and desires of the man were suddenly and completely changed; he stood before his friends and companions literally a new being, a new creation.

During his residence in Paris, where he gave full swing to his lusts, he was one day engaged in an intrigue with the wife of a surgeon or of an apothecary, with whom he had an appointment at a certain hour. In order to while away the interval, the major took up a book which his mother or aunt had slipped into his trunk long before, but which he had never opened. Whether the volume was Gurnall's *Christian Armour*, as one says, or Watson's *Christian Soldier*, as another says, can matter very little. Both most likely contain military phrases; it was these which arrested his attention, and the thought arose in his mind that he knew as much about them as the author could teach him. He soon found out, however, that a spiritual meaning was attached to them, and then he did not give his mind to receive that which his eye perceived. As he still held the book listlessly in his hand, he thought he saw a blaze of light fall on it, which at first he supposed must have been produced by some accident to the candles. But lifting up his eyes, he saw, to his extreme amazement, that there was before him, suspended in the air, a visible representation of the Lord Jesus

Christ upon the cross, surrounded on all sides with rays of glory. He was then impressed that a voice, or something equivalent to a voice, reached him, to this effect, for he was not confident as to the exact words, "O sinner! did I suffer this for thee, and are these thy returns?"

The pages of the book at which Gardiner was looking made no impression upon his mind, and yet a very extraordinary change passed over him from that very hour; a change as extraordinary as that which passed over Saul of Tarsus on his way to Damascus. He was renewed in the spirit of his mind; it was no mere outward change. He states that he perceived within himself a surprising alteration in the dispositions of his heart; licentious pleasures became his aversion; habituated as he had been to criminal indulgences, he now felt a strong abhorrence of them, although only a short time before he had regarded it as a simple impossibility that he could ever change his libidinous course of life.

The Life of Col. James Gardiner, Lucy Hutchinson

GEORGE GERRARD *An end to cynicism*
Former prisoner of war

Experience in transit prison camps in Belgium showed George Gerrard how human beings could be reduced by hunger, hardship and hopelessness to a condition of cynicism and pessimism. But once he reached England he gained contact with a Pentecostal church whose members were happy and showed genuine concern for their fellow human beings. It was in their love and concern, demonstrated to him in their homes, that he saw clearly the reality of the risen Christ.

He was invited to a meeting which proved the climax of his spiritual search. "Somehow that day I realised that to become, and to be, a Christian is not a moral evolution, where people strive to become good enough for an encounter with God. It is a revolution brought about by

104

God's Spirit when one's life is opened to Jesus Christ as God's Son and Saviour." That night, in the privacy of his cottage, he decided that he would no longer rely on people and on material things, but on Christ's guidance and salvation.

This brought him peace, but it also brought cynicism and aimlessness to an end; the world might be mad, but God and his love would ultimately triumph.

MARTIN GOLDSMITH   *Bullied*
Theologian of mission

When he was ten, Martin found a Bible in a trunk. He didn't even know it was a religious book, but it had an inscription showing that his Quaker godmother had given it to him as a christening present, and he began to read it, straight through like an adventure story. It took him about a year, whereupon he started at the beginning again.

He learned that God was a God of miracles, so he prayed for a miracle when he was being severely bullied at school. He simply asked for 24 hours of respite from the bullying. So total was the absence of bullying which God granted him, that he dedicated his life to God in the school chapel that same evening.

NIGEL GOODWIN   *On Wimbledon Common*
British actor

During a tent mission on Wimbledon Common, Nigel Goodwin became very uncomfortable. He was so frightened that he wanted to run from the tent and escape onto the Common. But he was drawn to attend several more meetings the following week. The preacher spoke about the story of blind Bartimaeus, and Goodwin felt as if his hands and heart had been tied all his life. Then he experienced a sense of peace in his whole body that he had never felt before. He believed in his heart that Jesus was the Son of God and that He alone could heal his sin. During that meeting in the tent on Wimbledon Common Goodwin knew that all this had been made possible by Jesus Christ's death on the cross. Jesus had opened his blind eyes.

JIM GOURLAY
Post Office worker

The Spirit comes

Jim Gourlay's wife surrounded him with Christian love, and prayed for him. Jim would go along to the Glasgow Baptist church with her, and enjoyed the hymns, but he did not know God or take in what the hymns and sermons were saying.

Then he had to work away from home, in London, and he found a small Pentecostal church where he heard an evangelistic sermon. He watched half a dozen young people respond to the appeal, and he prayed, "Father God, if this be your Spirit, may He come to me."

Back in his room, the following day, he had started writing his weekly letter home when he sensed the presence of God. He finished his letter with praise to God for His forgiveness, for accepting him as His child.

BILLY GRAHAM
American evangelist

Not just technique

Albert McMakin had packed as many people as possible into his truck so that they could attend a revivalist meeting. He wanted Billy to come too. But he played hard to get. So Albert told Billy that the preacher, Mordecai Ham, was not a sissy but rather a fighting preacher. When Albert then asked him to drive the truck for him Billy gave in and went along.

At the meeting was the biggest crowd of people Billy had ever seen in his life, and he listened to the whole proceedings completely spellbound. Mordecai Ham was certainly no disappointment, and he was no wimp either. In full cry Mordecai told that meeting in the Southern States of America about sin and about the Saviour, Jesus Christ. Billy recalls that he "had an almost embarrassing way of describing your sins and shortcomings and demanding, on pain of Divine Judgement, that you mend your ways. As I listened, I began to have thoughts I had never known before."

Billy went to bed that night very wistfully. The next day he could not wait to attend Mordecai's meeting. After his sixteenth birthday Billy did not know what was wrong with him, as he seemed to be so aimless in his life. Albert McMakin thought that he could detect that Billy was coming under conviction of sin, and rather than muscle in and talk to Billy about this, he decided to allow the Holy Spirit to carry on His work in Billy's heart.

Billy found Mordecai's habit of pointing his finger at his audience most disconcerting, and he even ducked behind the hat of the woman in front of him sometimes in order to avoid being pointed at. Then Billy decided to join the choir in his effort to avoid the evangelist's accusing finger.

But this move did not stop Billy having an overwhelming desire to commit himself to Christ. He can remember being convicted about sin in his life but he is not able to recall exactly what he felt so sinful about. But he does clearly remember that he felt weighed down by his burden of sin. He was scared about having to face God's judgement on his sin.

Billy continued going to the meetings, and eventually went forward at the appeal. He was now much more conscious of Christ than of his messenger Mordecai. He now knew that when Christ died on the cross He died for the sins of Billy Graham. When Mordecai asked people to go forward to the front as a sign that they wanted to follow Christ, the choir started to sing the hymn "Just as I am, without one plea ..." Billy was having a wrestling match in his conscience but managed to stay firmly glued to his seat throughout the hymn as others went forward to surround the pulpit area. Then the choir began to sing "'Almost persuaded' Christ to believe". The battle was over in Billy's heart. He left his seat and went forward. A tailor called J. D. Prevatt, whom Billy knew, came and spoke and prayed with Billy, who was already experiencing Christ's peace and joy. Seeing lots of people around him crying, Billy felt that his feelings were rather paltry in comparison. His father came over to him and hugged him tightly, giving thanks to God for the decision that Billy had taken that night.

Billy went to sleep wondering if this new experience would last. In the morning he found that everything he looked at seemed to be different and better, and he had no doubt in his heart that he had the Lord Jesus Christ with him.

FRED PRATT GREEN
Methodist minister and hymn-writer
In a Wesleyan chapel in Wallasey

Fred Green had a conversion experience after listening to a sermon about John Masefield's "Everlasting Mercy". He went to the chapel that his parents always went to in Wallasey and there became friends with the minister, whom he found to be both cultured and evangelistic. When Fred heard his sermon about the "Everlasting Mercy" he became a real follower of Christ, and before long he became a local preacher.

GREGORY
3rd-century missionary and Bishop of Neocaesarea
A persistent friend

Gregory was deeply affected by the death of his father when he was 14; he later came to believe that this was the beginning of his experience of God. He and his brother travelled to Palestine, hoping to go on to Beirut and study law there, but before they could continue their journey they met Origen, the great Christian philosopher.

Origen went to a lot of trouble to stop them travelling any further. He argued that if they were going to study they must "seek first of all to know themselves, what sort of people they are, and then the things that are truly good, that people should strive for, and then the things that are truly evil, from which people should run away". Day after day Origen persuaded them to stay and study with him; and he showed warm friendship to the lads.

Gregory wrote: "Love was set alight in us – both of the Holy Word (the most lovely of all objects of love, who draws everyone irresistibly to himself by his unutterable beauty) and of this man who was his friend and advocate. Having fallen in love, I was persuaded to give up everything else that people think is right and proper, even the study of law – indeed, my country and my friends, both the ones who were with me then and the ones I had left behind. As I saw it, there was just one thing worth pursuing, namely Christian truth, and this inspired man who was master of it."

Origen looked after Gregory and his brother as a gardener would look after his plants or a farmer his crops.

WILFRED GRENFELL
British medical missionary to Labrador

J. E. and C. T. Studd

It was in my second year, 1885, that, returning from an out-patient case one night, I turned into a large tent erected in a purlieu of Shadwell, the district to which I happened to have been called. It proved to be an evangelistic meeting of the then famous Moody and Sankey. It was so new to me that when a tedious prayer-bore began with a long oration, I started to leave. Suddenly the leader, whom I learned afterwards was D. L. Moody, called out to the audience, "Let us sing a hymn while our brother finishes his prayer." His practicality interested me, and I stayed the service out. When eventually I left, it was with a determination either to make religion a real effort to do as I thought Christ would do in my place as a doctor, or frankly abandon it. That could only have one issue while I still lived with a mother like mine. For she had always been my ideal of unselfish love.

So I decided to make the attempt, and later went down to hear the brothers J. E. and C. T. Studd speak at some subsidiary meeting of the Moody campaign. They were natural athletes, and I felt that I could listen to them. I could not have listened to a sensuous looking man, a man who was not a master of his own body, any more that I could to a precentor who, coming to sing the prayers at a college chapel dedication, I saw get drunk on sherry which he abstracted from the banquet table just before the service. Never shall I forget at the meeting of the Studd brothers, the audience being asked to stand up if they intended to try and follow Christ. It appeared a very sensible question to me, but I was amazed how hard I found it to stand up. At last one boy, out of a hundred or more in sailor rig, from an industrial or reformatory ship on the Thames, suddenly rose. It seemed to me such a wonderfully courageous act – for I knew perfectly what it would mean to him – that I immediately found myself on my feet, and went out feeling that I had crossed the Rubicon, and must do something to prove it.

The Story of a Labrador Doctor, Sir Wilfred Grenfell,
Hodder & Stoughton, 1925, p. 30

WILLIAM GRIMSHAW   *Glorious vision*
18th-century vicar of Haworth, Yorkshire

Before the Brontës brought fame to the Yorkshire village of Haworth, an extraordinary minister had brought it notoriety as the centre of evangelistic preaching so bold and persistent that it thoroughly annoyed the neighbouring (less effective) clergy.

    William Grimshaw had been a very worldly parson elsewhere. He used to hunt, fish, play cards, get drunk and preach borrowed sermons. If anyone came to him for spiritual advice he would be likely to tell them to stop thinking gloomy thoughts and go and enjoy themselves. But then he started praying: four times a day, which he continued to do till his death. He started studying the Bible seriously. He read properly two books which he had been given at his ordination – *Precious Remedies against Satan's Devices* by the puritan Thomas Brooks, and John Owen's *On Justification*. The Bible and John Owen between them brought about his conversion – his servant found him one Sunday still on his knees at five o'clock in the morning; he continued throughout the day to give every available moment to prayer. He fainted, but when he came to he said he had had "a glorious vision of the third heaven". He had a new sense of God's forgiveness, a new assurance of salvation, and when he conducted the afternoon service it started at two o'clock but went on until seven.

After this, Grimshaw was a changed man, his preaching informed by an understanding of the Bible so different that he said it was as if God had taken his old Bible up to heaven and sent him another one in return.

The call to Haworth came in that same year, and Grimshaw also preached in all the surrounding area: apart from his own parish, he had a two-week schedule of itinerant preaching which involved him preaching about fourteen times in his "lazy" week and often thirty times in his "busy" week.

The Archbishop of York had complaints from ministers whose parishes were visited by Grimshaw, so he summoned the man to the palace.

"How many communicants did you find on coming to Haworth?" asked the archbishop.

"Twelve, my lord."

"How many have you now?"

"In the winter between three and four hundred, according to the weather. In the summer sometimes nearer twelve hundred."

The archbishop was wise enough to draw the obvious conclusion: "We can find no fault with Mr Grimshaw, seeing that he is instrumental in bringing so many persons to the Lord's Table."

MICHELE GUINNESS
Jewish convert, author and TV producer

Mystery opened

Michele felt as if God looked down on her life from heaven and was displeased with her. She wondered if God would ever forgive her and if life could ever be different from what she knew.

She found herself on a school trip to York to see the Mystery Plays. Little did she realize that these plays were nothing less than medieval interpretations of the stories contained in the Bible. The plays helped Michele to understand that the New Testament continued the message of the Old Testament.

During one of the plays a cross was lifted up high into the air with Christ on it, his arms stretched out. Something snapped inside Michele. She clearly understood what she had been reading in the Bible. She wanted to jump up and shout out, "That's it! I see it now! That's why Christ had to die, for me, for my sins, so that I can be forgiven and have eternal life." Instead of doing any of this she gripped her bench tightly.

Michele is a little lost for words to fully explain all that took place in her life that evening. But she became certain of one thing. She would never be the same person again.

DAVID HAMILTON
Former Ulster Volunteer Force paramilitary

Converted in prison

David Hamilton threw a Christian tract out of his cell, as he had so little interest in religion. But two days later he was taken by surprise. Something strange had happened to him. Christ had broken into his life.

He now believes that he was prayed into God's kingdom. Hamilton did not know it at the time, but he later found out that an 83-year-old lady, a friend of his mother, together with his mother had been praying for him over the previous year and a half.

Hamilton recalls how he spent his first two days as a

Christian in prison. He stayed awake at night and thought of each prisoner and prayed for them one at a time.

During the hunger strike in the Maze prison, Hamilton and the other Christians fasted and prayed. They asked to intervene in the darkness of the prison.

God heard their prayers in a most remarkable way. Prisoners in different parts of the prison just picked up the Bibles in their cells and read them. They had conversations about Christianity with nobody. Yet they become followers of Christ.

When Hamilton entered the Maze prison in 1977 he know of only one Christian. Upon his release six years later he knew of 120 committed Christians.

AUDREY HARPER
Converted witch

Lord over witchcraft

Audrey was being asked to renounce her witchcraft, and to repent of having been a witch. She did this, but was it the spirits making her lie?

It was all plain sailing until Audrey was asked to confess that Jesus Christ is the Lord.

She managed to repeat the words parrot-fashion: "Jesus Christ is the Lord." She even managed to do the same with the sentence: "Yes, I confess Jesus Christ is my Lord."

But the storm broke when she was asked to repeat: "Jesus Christ is Lord over witchcraft." Audrey was not herself. She went for her Christian friend's throat with her hands. But something stopped her. It was as if an invisible barrier had suddenly been erected between them. It looked as if Audrey had smashed into a wall.

With a combination of anger and sorrow Audrey tried to leave, but after taking a few steps towards the door she fell down as if she was dead. A three-hour-long battle for Audrey's soul followed. After that, to everybody's evident relief, Audrey did confess that Jesus Christ was her Lord and that He had forgiven her for all her evil ways: witchcraft, murder, pornography and theft. Jesus was now Audrey's Lord in every part of her life.

HOWELL HARRIS
18th-century Welsh evangelist
A melting heart

The village schoolteacher in Talgarth, Brecon, was not really interested in the schoolboys. He was more interested in drinking and gossiping and pretty girls. He used to pray to God, but he still carried on with his worldly life.

Then on the Sunday before Easter in 1735 he went to church and heard the vicar say: "You plead your unfitness to come to the Holy Communion. Let me tell you, that if you are not fit to come to the Lord's Supper, you are not fit to come to church, you are not fit to live; you are not fit to die." Harris instantly resolved to prepare himself properly for the next Sunday's Communion service.

As he repeated the confession in that Easter Day service – 'we are heartily sorry for all our misdoings; the remembrance of them is grievous unto us, the burden of them is intolerable' – he knew that he was not being honest with God. He had no such sense of sin.

In the following weeks he tried to keep his thoughts on God, and through reading a book on the Ten Commandments he abandoned reliance on his own efforts and came to find salvation through Christ alone. He also read, in a devotional book, the words, "If we would go to the sacrament simply believing in the Lord Jesus Christ, we should receive forgiveness of all our sins."

On Whit Sunday, genuinely repenting and firmly believing, he came again to the Holy Communion. "I was convinced by the Holy Ghost that Christ died for me, and that all my sins were laid on Him. I was now acquitted at the bar of justice, and in my conscience. This evidenced itself to be true faith by the peace, joy, watchfulness, hatred to sin, and fear of offending God that followed it," he wrote.

Later, praying privately in church, he felt his heart melting "like wax before the fire, with love to God my Saviour; and also felt, not only love and peace but a longing to be dissolved and be with Christ. There was a cry in my soul which I was totally unacquainted with before – 'Abba Father!' I could not help calling God my Father. I *knew* that I was His child and that He loved and heard me."

He felt compelled, despite his innate reticence, to share his experience with others. Getting little response from the clergy when he complained about the moral degeneracy of the place, he began reading to neighbours, then ministering to the sick, then visiting his old friends, urging them to amend their ways, and then became a house-to-house evangelist in his own parish and further afield. Many people came to listen to him, the practice of family worship was revived and many more people started taking Communion.

ROBERT HARRIS
17th-century minister and head of
Trinity College, Oxford

Compulsory prayers

He showed a more than ordinary desire of learning, and having but little help either from the Principal [of Magdalen Hall, Oxford], or his Tutor, he followed his private studies with the more earnestness; yet all this while he enquired little into the ways and truths of God.

His tutor not long after leaving the Hall, he earnestly solicited the Principal, that he might be committed to the care of one Mr Goffe of Magdalen College, who was noted for a very good logician and disputant, but withal he was accounted a puritan, which made the Principal (who was popishly affected) to dissuade his choice; but he (not out of love to religion, but learning) persisted in his desires, and prevailed.

Mr Goffe having thus received him into his charge, required him, that with the rest of his fellow-pupils, he should join in reading the scriptures, repetition of sermons and prayer; which new course, he being unaccustomed to, was somewhat troubled at it, observing that none of the seniors embraced that way, and yet it was such as he knew not how to contradict. This caused him oft to betake himself to his private prayers, wherein he begged of God, either to discover to him the falsehood, if his tutor had any design upon him to corrupt him, or if this course were pleasing to God, that then he would confirm him in it; and it pleased God after a while so to resolve him, that he bought a Bible, and with indefatigable pains he applied himself to the reading of that, and other good authors in divinity ...

He was a man that had much acquaintance with God, much communion with him in private meditation and prayer, accounting those his best days wherein he enjoyed most converse with him.

In the time of his sickness, one asking him how he did, "Oh," saith he, "this hath been a sweet day, I have had sweet communion with God in Jesus Christ." He was not like them who are all for promises and privileges, though in the meantime they neglect duties: he made them his exercise, but not his Christ ...

The Lord was pleased to work upon him in the primrose of his life, though he certainly knew not, either the preacher or the sermon whereby he was converted. His course was in the days of his strictest examination to set down in writing his evidences for heaven, sometimes in propositions from scripture; other sometimes in syllogisms, and these he often subscribed to in a book that he kept for that very purpose. But these evidences were best read by others in the course of his life, by his exact walking with God in piety, charity, humility, patience, and dependence upon him. He was far unlike to those who sit in Moses' chair, and teach what they themselves practise not.... His life was a commentary upon his doctrine, and his practice the counterpane of his sermons ... He lived religion, whilst many only make it the subject of their discourse.

A Collection of the Lives of Ten Eminent Divines, Samuel Clarke, Miller, 1662, pp. 275, 302–303

WILLIAM HASLAM
19th-century minister of Baldhu, Cornwall

Converted by his own sermon

[A clerical friend had challenged the genuineness of Mr Haslam's faith, and for some time Haslam suffered darkness and despair, feeling unfit to take a service even. He went to church one Sunday expecting only to read the prayer-book service, and then decided he would at least make a few remarks about the gospel passage set for the day.]

So I went up into the pulpit and gave out my text. I took it from the gospel of the day – "What think ye of Christ?" (Matthew 22:42).

As I went on to explain the passage, I saw that the Pharisees and scribes did not know that Christ was the Son of God, or that He was come to save them. They were looking for a king, the son of David, to reign over them as they were. Something was telling me, all the time, "You are no better than the Pharisees yourself – you do not believe that He is the Son of God, and that He is come to save you, any more than they did." I do not remember all I said, but I felt a wonderful light and joy coming into my soul, and I was beginning to see what the Pharisees did not. Whether it was something in my words, or my manner, or my look, I know not; but all of a sudden a local preacher, who happened to be in the congregation, stood up, and putting up his arms, shouted out in Cornish manner, "The parson is converted! the parson is converted! Hallelujah!" and in another moment his voice was lost in the shouts and praises of three or four hundred of the congregation. Instead of rebuking this extraordinary "brawling", as I should have done in a former time, I joined in the outburst of praise; and to make it more orderly, I gave out the Doxology – "Praise God, from whom all blessings flow" – and the people sang it with heart and voice, over and over again.

Diary, William Haslam, Brentano's, 1895

FRANCES RIDLEY HAVERGAL
"Take my life"
19th-century hymn-writer

Frances Ridley Havergal's mother died when Frances was only eleven, yet she left her daughter words which were to carry her through all her life: "Pray to God to prepare you for all that He is preparing for you."

Fanny's headmistress was shortly to retire, and had resolved to see each one of her pupils converted before she left. "She prayed and spoke with us, together and individually, with a fervour which I have never seen equalled," wrote Frances later. But Fanny seemed as far from the Kingdom as ever when the end of term came.

A schoolfriend, too, "begged me to go to Jesus to tell Him I wanted to love Him and could not, and then He would teach me to".

In her old age, Miss Havergal said: "The words of wise and even eminent men have since fallen on my ear, but few have brought the dewy refreshment to my soul which the simple loving words of my heaven-taught schoolfellow did."

Another help to her in her childhood was her new stepmother, to whom she turned when she wanted to find God's forgiveness. "Could you not commit your soul to Him, to your Saviour, Jesus?" asked her stepmother.

"I *could*, surely," replied the girl.

"Then and there," she later recalled, "I committed my soul to the Saviour – and earth and heaven seemed bright from that moment."

There were to be many more periods of doubt and fear. She sensed in others a spiritual satisfaction she did not herself experience, and when she was 36 she entered into correspondence with the author of a tract she had read, which culminated in her finding new blessing. "I was shown that 'the blood of Jesus Christ His Son cleanseth us from all sin,' and then it was made plain to me that He who had thus cleansed had power to keep me clean; so I just utterly yielded myself to Him, and utterly trusted Him to keep me."

Shortly after that, she wrote the hymn:

> Take my life, and let it be
> Consecrated, Lord, to Thee;
> Take my moments and my days,
> Let them flow in ceaseless praise.

BRYN HAWORTH   *Shouting at God*
Rock musician

Living in an isolated part of Wales, Bryn Haworth could go for long country walks, literally shouting at God to reveal Himself. He had given up the rock lifestyle of drink and drugs and had begun to see that "what I was saying were things my friends had said ... I just didn't know who I was. I suddenly realised that what I was looking for wasn't in me and that it must be outside."

Bryn and his wife were intrigued by a television programme in which people were seen really praising God, and soon the couple found themselves going into a tent crusade where they heard the Gospel for the first time. "I walked out of that tent and I looked at the sky and I thought, I'm home."

DANNY HEARN   *Challenge*
England international rugby player

As a schoolboy, Danny had begun thinking about Christianity, but he couldn't understand what "being a Christian" meant. He prayed, "Please, God, make me a Christian", but then he got caught up in academic and sporting pursuits and left no time for Christianity.

At Oxford, when he was doing his postgraduate Education course, Danny encountered a clergyman who challenged him. He started seeing this man privately before sports training sessions, and he came near to accepting the challenge.

119

He eventually did become a Christian, through a friend on the staff at Haileybury, where he had started teaching. But now, with a place on the England team and the possibility of becoming its captain, Danny was worried lest his faith detract from his public image. He need not have worried: "I found a new direction and a new circle of friends and the peace that every Christian knows."

In many ways he decided not to change his lifestyle – he would witness through being known as a Christian rugby player and teacher. That wasn't quite how it worked out, because 18 months later Danny had an accident which left him paralysed from the neck down. But through his humiliating dependence on others he was able to learn more about his dependence on God.

MICHAEL HEATON-ELLIS
Racehorse trainer

*A crippling
riding accident*

God was just part of the English public-school order of things for Mikie Heaton-Ellis; but he turned to thoughts of God when he was facing difficulties.

His life appeared to be enormously successful: he became a handsome young army officer with plenty of money, plenty of girl-friends and plenty of ability at sport and academic studies. But he was not entirely satisfied with his life even then.

The big blow came when, as a keen racehorse jockey and trainer, he suffered a riding accident which left him permanently paralysed from the chest down. It was some time before he recognized that the accident had made him bitter against God, and that he had been thinking of God as the provider, rather than as the Lord he should be serving. A Christian friend and a vicar helped him to work through the implications, and to study the Bible. He decided to ask Jesus to take over his life – in fact, he prayed the same prayer of commitment several times in the space of a few days, to reinforce it.

His marriage had broken up, and for a time he hoped God would bring his wife back to him; however, he had to learn that this was not to be, just as the healing of his body was not to be. He came to see, though, how God could bring good out of disaster.

JAMES HERVEY   *Reading St Paul*
18th-century writer of popular religious books

Hervey could not work out how the doctrine of justification was to be understood. George Whitefield wrote from America: "Let me advise dear Mr Hervey, laying aside all prejudices, to read and pray over St Paul's Epistles to the Romans and Galatians, and then tell me what he thinks of the doctrine." This Hervey did, and in time he was brought to a personal understanding.

"You are pleased to ask, How the Holy Ghost convinced me of self-righteousness, and drove me out of my false rests?" he wrote to Whitefield. "Indeed, sir, I cannot precisely tell. The light was not instantaneous, but gradual. It did not flash upon my soul, but arose like the dawning day."

His whole attitude now changed: "I now desire to work in my blessed Master's service, not *for*, but *from* salvation." And as part of his work he wrote books such as *Meditations Among the Tombs*, which were designed to bring the Gospel message to the mid-18th-century literary world.

GLENN HODDLE   *The birthplace of Jesus*
England international footballer

When Glenn Hoddle played football for Tottenham Hotspur he went to a dinner which had been arranged by the organization "Christians in Sport". It had been planned that he should sit next to Cliff Richard. As a result of this Glenn began to read the Bible.

Six years later Glenn found himself in Israel. It was part of the England squad's warm-up preparations for the World Cup games in Mexico. In Israel they were taken to Bethlehem and saw the likely birthplace of Jesus. Until then Glenn had thought that Jesus was little more than a story. But seeing his birthplace, Glenn became convinced that Jesus had really lived on this earth.

After he returned home he started to read his Bible again and to talk to Christians, including Harry Hughes, who ran the Spurs shop. Through reading his Bible Glenn found that the questions he had about life were answered, and so he committed his life to the living Lord Jesus Christ.

JACQUES HOPKINS   *Converted at sea*
Singer

In World War I, Jacques Hopkins served on a ship under a captain who gave thanks to God at the dinner table – and who prayed privately for the conversion of this lad with the wonderful voice. He not only prayed – he preached, and having preached he spent time talking with Hopkins. He opened his much-used Bible and showed him how God was willing to forgive him because of the death of His Son, who accepted the punishment which the sinner deserved. Everlasting life was on offer, and Hopkins accepted the offer. The captain prayed for the boy, and the boy prayed, "Lord, save me."

There was an old lady who was a friend of that captain, and the very same day she had been praying all through the day, thousands of miles away, not understanding why the captain needed prayer but knowing that he did.

SELWYN HUGHES *Peace and joy*
Preacher, pastor and writer of the *Every Day*
***With Jesus* Bible reading notes**

Selwyn set out for the local dance. Before arriving at the
dance hall he had to pass by the local Assemblies of God mission hall. He could not believe his ears. He heard the voice
that belonged to his dad, and his dad was praying for him and
for his conversion. Selwyn was overwhelmed. He recalls,
"Somehow as he prayed his voice penetrated my soul."

None of this caused any immediate or dramatic change in
Selwyn's life. Some time later he head a sermon preached by
a visiting speaker at the mission hall. Selwyn had heard him
preach many times before, and he was expecting to be
thoroughly bored by the service, but instead it seemed to
Selwyn that on this occasion the preacher's face was practi-
cally shining with light, and all his words went right home to
Selwyn's heart. The preacher said: "God wants you to be
saved tonight ... come to Jesus who will save you from your
sins and give you peace and joy that will last for ever."

Selwyn could hold back his tears no longer. He cried his
heart out as he prayed his prayer of repentance. He was a
relieved man. He was a forgiven man. Jesus Christ was now
his Saviour. Selwyn now knew that he had been saved.

SELINA, COUNTESS *The limits of charity*
OF HUNTINGDON
Early supporter of Methodism

At the age of nine, Selina followed a funeral procession to the
grave, and was deeply moved. "With many tears she earnestly
implored God, on the spot, that whenever he should be
pleased to take her away, he would deliver her from all her
fears, and give her a happy departure." She seems to have
returned both literally and metaphorically to that graveside
on many occasions.

After her marriage, aged 21, she did many good works,

having the idea that in her exalted position it became her to show piety and charity. "Her sentiments were liberal, and her charity profuse," says a biographer; "she was prudent in her conduct, and courteous in her deportment; she was a diligent enquirer after truth, and a strenuous advocate for virtue; she was frequent in her sacred meditations, and was a regular attendant at public worship." Naturally, she got a good reputation, and she therefore became conceited. "While the Countess was taken up in congratulating herself upon her own fancied eminence in piety, she was an absolute stranger to that inward and universal change of heart, wrought by the gracious operations of the Spirit of God."

Her sister-in-law was converted, however, and eager to share her faith. Talking to the Countess, she said that since her conversion she had been happy as an angel – and the Countess knew herself a stranger to such peace and joy. Greater self-discipline brought no consolation, and a serious illness reminded her of her childhood experience. Then she had nowhere to turn but to Christ, knowing that her good deeds were worthless. From that day she became a transformed person, not hesitating to align herself with the Methodists, Moravians and evangelical Anglican preachers who were largely despised, and giving a fortune as well as her personal friendship in support of them. "Oh, that I might be more and more useful to the souls of my fellow-creatures," she wrote. "I want to be every moment all life, all zeal, all activity for God, and ever on the stretch for closer communion with him."

BRIAN IRVINE
Scottish football star
As a result of a car journey

Brian was brought up in a Christian home, but going to church meant very little to him. He vividly remembers his conversion experience. At the time he was studying two nights a week, football training two nights a week, playing a match on Saturdays and working for the Clydesdale Bank during the day. He was travelling in a car on the way to a football match at Falkirk. The conversation turned to what the meaning of life was, and somebody else in the car said that he thought that Jesus Christ would return to this earth. This made Brian read his Bible at home that evening. Suddenly the Bible came alive to Brian and he knew for himself that he was loved by God and that his sins had been dealt with by Jesus when He died on the cross. That night was Brian's Damascus Road. That night he became a Christian.

TOCKICHI ISHII
Japanese murderer

Two lady prison visitors

Tockichi Ishii was renowned for being a pitiless criminal. He had murdered men, women and even children during his career in crime. After he had eventually been captured, sentenced and imprisoned two Canadian ladies visited his prison.

He refused to speak to them when they came to his cell. He merely stared at them with the eyes of a wild animal.

More in hope than in expectation, the two ladies left him a Bible in his cell, just in case he should read it. Ishii did read this Bible. He read the story of the crucifixion of Jesus as the evangelist Matthew records it. This changed the murderer's life. When the jailer came to lead the doomed man to the scaffold, he found that a new Ishii, happy and pleasant, had replaced the sour hateful old Ishii. This murderer had been born again and his smiling radiance was proof of his rebirth.

MICHELLE JANIS
Researcher

Jewish family

Born in a Chicago Jewish family, Michelle thought little about God until she was at college, where she found numerous friends who were Christians. She envied their peace and joy, and she started going to their Bible studies, even though she didn't want Jesus. She was afraid of death, and had felt the love of her Christian friends, so she prayed to God to prove to her that Jesus was His Son. "All of a sudden I was put in touch with what I call divine appointments," she says. "I mean, I felt the Spirit of the Lord."

She was still apprehensive, because of half-remembered stories of an Old Testament God who destroyed people, but she had a sense of being filled with the Holy Spirit. She also had a vision of the throne of God, with Christ at the right hand of the Father – a theological idea she had not come across at the time.

Her mother was appalled when told of Michelle's conversion; her father took it well at first, thinking it was just a phase she would grow out of. But she didn't grow out of it. A few years later she took her mother with her on a trip to Israel, and four months after their return her mother rang up to say that she too had become a Christian. Within a few months, Michelle's brother and sister had also been converted.

WILLIAM JAY
19th-century Nonconformist preacher

"Like rain upon the mown grass"

Some persons love to talk of their being born again, and of their being made new creatures, with a kind of physical certainty and exactness; and refer to their conversion, not as the real commencement of a work which is to continue increasing through life, but as something which may be viewed as a distant and unique experience, immediately produced, originated and finished at once; and perfectly determinable, as to its time and place and mode of accomplishment; but I hope this is not necessary, for I have no such narrative or register to afford.

The private dwelling which Mr Tanner had purchased and licensed was first used for worship on the Saturday evening. I attended. The singing, the extemporaneousness of the

126

address, and the apparent affection and earnestness of the speaker, peculiarly affected me: and what he said of "the faithful saying, and worthy of all acceptation, that Jesus Christ came into the world to save sinners," was like rain upon the mown grass, or cold water to a thirsty soul. I scarcely slept that night for weeping, and for joy.

Autobiography, William Jay, 1854, pp. 21–23

JEROME   *Classics or Christ?*
4th-century Bible translator

As a young man Jerome had one love – the classics. He would have happily spent his whole life in studying them.

One night he had a dream which changed the course of his life. In his dream he was taken up to heaven and brought before the throne of God. There he was told off for spending so much time in studying the classics and so little time in studying Christian books. God's voice spoke to him in his dream: "You think more of Cicero than you do of Christ. You are a Ciceronian, not a Christian."

After that dream he determined to spend his life in studying the Bible. Soon after this, in AD 382, the Pope summoned him and told him to revise some of the manuscripts of the Psalms and to translate the Bible into Latin. Jerome spent the next 22 years of his life doing this. His translation was known as the Vulgate and became the one authorized version of the Bible until the Reformation.

ALEXANDER JOHN   *Pressurized*
Yugoslav pop singer

Alexander hated his mother's personal belief in God. He felt pressurized by the church friends she invited round to try and convert him. They didn't ask him what he thought, but expected him to accept their own thoughts, and this he found arrogant.

He would often end up swearing on these occasions, making his mother cry, and he knew he had no power of himself to do what he wanted to do.

Then a relative of one of the other church members came to stay for a week. He was about Alexander's own age, and was a Christian, but he did not talk about his faith until Alexander asked. Because the subject had not been forced, Alexander let him talk, and when the visitor had left Alexander started to read the Bible. He was enormously attracted by the personality of Jesus and wanted to be like Him.

One night he decided he would try praying – something he had never done before. He knelt, as a sign of humility, a sign that he was incapable of dealing with his own problems. And that was how, at 17 years of age, he became a Christian.

AUDREY WETHERELL JOHNSON *In despair*
Founder of the Bible Study Fellowship

Audrey was born in Leicester, England, and enjoyed all the benefits of being brought up in a loving Christian home. But when she went to France for her further education she was overwhelmed by the ideas of secular philosophy, and she abandoned her basic belief that the Bible was a book that could be trusted completely.

She kept her agnosticism to herself, as she did not wish to upset her family. She could not stomach hearing any sermons about the cross of Christ or the blood of Christ.

Now that she had thrown overboard her Christian way of looking at life, she was sinking into deep despair within herself. She began to think that it did not matter what one believed in this life, since everything ends at death anyway. One night the following verses from the Bible forced her to rethink everything about her eternal destiny: "I am the resurrection, and the life: he that believeth in me, though he were dead, yet shall he live: And whosoever liveth and believeth in me, though he were dead, yet shall he live" (John 11:25–26). She prayed to God that she might understand the meaning of these words. Her prayer was dramatically answered. She was greatly surprised that she had a revelation from God about who Jesus was. She thinks that it was similar to the one the apostle Paul received and which he referred to when he wrote, "It pleased God ... to reveal his Son to me" (Galatians 1:15–16). Even though Audrey was still unable to fathom the mystery of the Incarnation, she was completely satisfied that it was true because God had revealed this to her. She promptly knelt down and with joyful tears worshipped her newly discovered Lord and Saviour.

She was later to found the Bible Study Fellowship. Its work still continues throughout the world, with over 800 Bible study groups linked to it.

E. STANLEY JONES   *Deadly serious*
Missionary in India

Stanley Jones wanted the kingdom of God. He wanted to be reconciled with his Father in heaven. But to start with he simply belonged to the church instead. His mother thought he had become a Christian, but it was not long before her son's new religious feelings faded, and he became just the same as he had been before he joined the church.

Two years later, an evangelist came – a former alcoholic whose faith was real and visible. Stanley wanted what that evangelist had, and he was deadly serious about it. On the third night of his visit, Stanley knelt and prayed before going to the meeting: he prayed to Jesus to save him that night, and Jesus answered that prayer. Light came into his darkness. In new hope Stanley found that he was sure that Jesus was going to do it. Afterwards he saw that in fact Jesus had already "done it", but the new convert expected it to happen in church.

PAUL JONES
Pop star
Caspar David Friedrich's paintings

The little-known 18th-century painter Caspar David Friedrich set Paul Jones' heart and mind alight. Through studying these paintings Paul realized that the artist must have had a great love for Jesus Christ.

This changed Paul's deeply critical views on Christianity. So he was even prepared to attend an evangelistic meeting led by Luis Palau, even though years earlier he had publicly poured scorn on Billy Graham's and Cliff Richard's attempts to communicate Christ at such campaigns. With Fiona Hindley, who is now his wife, he gave his life to Christ at that evangelistic meeting held at Queen's Park Rangers football ground.

JUSTIN
2nd-century teacher and martyr
"A fire was lit in my soul"

Justin studied with one of the Stoic philosophers, but the Stoic did not believe in God. He went to a Peripatetic, but despised his concern with the fees to be charged for lessons. The Pythagorean teacher required so many subjects as an entry requirement for the course that Justin felt he could not wait long enough to acquire them all. He enjoyed making progress with an eminent Platonist teacher, and was expecting to get a vision of God any day now, when he went off to think quietly by himself in a remote spot and met an old man who was a Christian.

This man introduced Justin to the prophets, who did not "set out their accounts with formal argument, but as witnesses of the truth worthy of belief, as if they were above all formal argument". He recommended Justin to pray for the enlightenment which God alone can give.

"Immediately a fire was lit in my soul," reports Justin, "and a desire for the prophets seized me and for those men who are friends of Christ."

TOYOHIKO KAGAWA   *"Make me like Christ"*
Japanese Christian

Kagawa, at the age of 15, went to learn English from a Christian missionary in Japan, and the Gospel of Luke was one of the texts he had to study. He read about the things Jesus did for people, and when he read how Jesus had been crucified he was amazed. "Oh God," he prayed, "make me like Christ."

He was reluctant at first to seek baptism, because his uncle was paying for his education and Kagawa was worried about his uncle's reaction when he heard that his nephew had become a Christian. But his Christian teachers pointed out that this was cowardly, so he asked for baptism, and his uncle did not object – until Kagawa announced that he wanted to be ordained.

He went on to live and work for the poorest people, to work for the state to allow trade unions, to preach Christ in Japan and abroad, to write 150 books and to denounce first his own country and then the USA and the Allies for their pursuit of war.

BYANG HENRY KATO   *Mission school*
Nigerian fetish worshipper

When he was just a few months old, Kato was dedicated to be a juju priest. The very fact that he survived childhood, when seven out of his eight younger siblings died, showed clearly to the local Jaba people how powerful fetish worship was, or how the Devil was looking after his priest-to-be.

It was not until after he had undergone the tribal initiation ceremony that Kato first took an interest in Christianity. A Christian boy invited him to a mission school, and he kept on going to hear Bible verses being chanted and Bible stories being told. A teacher invited the boys to accept Jesus as their Saviour, and Kato did so, with the simple faith of a child.

There followed a period of constant failure, but when Kato was in his teens there was a Christian revival in the land, and

131

as a result of this Kato promised to serve Jesus actively. He who had been expected to become a pagan priest was later to travel to England to study for a degree in Christian theology.

KAZAINAK — *"Tell me that again"*
Robber in Greenland

Kazainak was a chief robber and a very violent man. A Christian missionary read him the story of Christ's sufferings and death, and this made Kazainak ask what Christ had done to deserve all this punishment. He wondered if He had been a robber or a murderer perhaps. Kazainak was bemused to discover that Christ was neither a robber nor a murderer and had done nothing wrong at all.

The robber was intrigued to find out why Christ should then have had to suffer. The Christian missionary explained it to Kazainak in this way. Christ had done nothing wrong, but Kazainak has done lots wrong. Christ did not rob anybody, but Kazainak has robbed many people. Christ murdered nobody, but Kazainak murdered his brother. Christ suffered so that Kazainak might not suffer. Christ died so that Kazainak does not have to die.

"Tell me that again," responded the robber. Then the hard-bitten sinner turned from his evil life and became a humble follower of the Lord Jesus Christ.

CINDY KENT — *"A different person"*
Singer

Cindy became a Christian when she was 14, through the youth work of a chapel attended by her sister and a school friend. Cindy said, "Mum and dad reckoned I was a different person!"

Later, she drifted away from the chapel and allowed folk music to take over the place which Christianity should have occupied in her life. She was isolated in the world of entertainment until she heard that Cliff Richard was also a believer. Then she started making an effort to get involved in church life again, and she joined other Christians in doing Gospel concerts, evangelistic meetings and so on.

GRAHAM KERR
Marriage transformed
Television cookery expert ("the Galloping Gourmet")

A very strained marriage was transformed after Graham Kerr returned from one of his TV trips. He ordered his wife about mercilessly, but got none of the usual hostile reaction. Nor was Treena telling *him* what to do and what not to do.

An accidental meeting with another person gave Graham the unbelievable news that Treena had, in his absence, been baptized. "I suppose you want me to become a Christian?" he asked. "No, not really," replied Treena, who knew she'd pushed him enough in the past and on this matter could only witness quietly.

As his wife's commitment deepened, Graham's unease deepened too. "What's the matter?" asked Treena one day. "It's Him," replied Graham, pointing heavenwards.

Nothing changed immediately, but on his next trip away from home Graham tried to read the Bible and pray.

"God, if you're there at all, for goodness' sake, what do I say to get through to you? How do I get the lightness that Treena has? How can I get away from this despondency, this nothingness that I've got?" And he thought of the cross and said, "Jesus, I love you."

A few days later Graham returned home and for the first time prayed with his wife. "We were born again and married again," he says. And in their renewed marriage the competitiveness has gone. If danger approaches, they hold each other's hands and look at each other – and see Jesus.

GEORGE KILNER
London barrister

Relatives prayed

George Kilner had a good tenor voice, and on one occasion was persuaded to sing with his choir at a D. L. Moody evangelistic meeting at the Metropolitan Tabernacle in south London. The church was packed full, and the friend who had asked Kilner to sing knew that somewhere in the building Kilner's mother and sister were sitting praying for their beloved George.

After the singing, Kilner wanted to leave. He was pleased to have been able to help out, but he had an appointment. His friend had other ideas, however – and knew that Kilner was really apprehensive about the sermon. Would George please stay on to sing again at the end?

And so Kilner stayed, and listened to Moody's sermon on the plan of salvation and the work of Christ. He stayed on for the meeting afterwards and sat opposite Moody.

Moody began: "Well, you've heard all about it. Won't you come? We're here for business and want to know which of you will close with the offer of salvation and take Jesus Christ for his Saviour. Don't be afraid; He is waiting for you. Now, what man has courage to rise and take the Lord Jesus as his Saviour?"

Kilner was the first to get to his feet. He walked over to the evangelist, held out his hand and said, "I'll take Him, Mr Moody."

ALAN KNOTT
English test cricketer

Kensington Temple

Up to 1973 Alan Knott had spent his time thinking up reasons against Christianity. Then in the autumn of 1973 he found himself with his wife Jan in the Californian home of their friends the Severns. The Severns prayed that Alan and Jan would invite the Lord Jesus Christ into their lives. Although they did not do so then, Alan did follow Billy

Severns' advice and started to view Christianity more positively, thinking of reasons for believing and not reasons for disbelieving.

During the summer of 1974 the Knotts visited Jan's brother after he had been in a road accident from which he was expected to die. Alan and Jan prayed for Jan's brother and, against all the odds, he recovered.

The Severns had introduced Jan and Alan to Eldin Corsie, the pastor of the Kensington Temple in London. At the end of a Sunday service Jan and Alan went to the front of the church in response to the invitation to do so if they wanted to become Christians. This was something that Alan knew he had to do and this was the moment he actually decided to ask Christ into his life.

FRANCESCO LACUEVA
Roman Catholic convert

"Slow, difficult and confusing"

Lacueva says that his conversion was "slow, difficult and confusing".

Lacueva was Professor of Special Dogmatic Theology at a Roman Catholic seminary in Tarazona, close to Zaragoza. But he found that he had a major intellectual problem when he tried to objectively study Christian doctrines in the light of the Word of God and the faith of the Primitive Church: he could not square his findings with the traditional teachings of the Catholic Church. He was unable to answer the probing questions on these matters which his students fired at him. Lacueva drifted into agnosticism and then sank into atheism.

Lacueva wrote to a friend, sharing his problem. His friend replied to his letter and told him about conversion to God, and about the need for everybody to accept Jesus as their own personal Redeemer.

This letter struck a chord deep in Lacueva's soul. The letter was followed by parcels of evangelical literature, which helped the professor to study the Word of God carefully.

In his last few months in Spain he preached the Gospel

from Roman Catholic pulpits, which was appreciated, even though his hearers were unaware that they were listening to Protestant doctrine. Lacueva had come to put his faith for his own personal salvation in Jesus Christ and would trust Him in life and in death.

GERALD LANDER   *Through D. L. Moody*
American missionary bishop in China

When the American evangelist D. L. Moody started to preach at Cambridge University, his New England accent was immediately made fun of. Moody himself also feared that they would deride him for his fifth-grade education and his many American mannerisms.

Gerald Lander had been in the front row at this meeting and had joyfully joined in teasing this earnest evangelist. He even told one of the student organizers of the meeting that if "uneducated men will come to teach the varsity, they deserve to be snubbed". However, Lander was in a different frame of mind by the following morning. He took his courage in both hands and went round to the hotel where Moody was staying and went to his room. There he apologized to Moody and even read out a letter of apology from other students who had ridiculed Moody so mercilessly the night before. Moody listened carefully to all of this and then had a long chat with Lander. He ended up by challenging him and his friends to come to his next meeting to prove their sincerity.

Lander did attend Moody's next meeting, and the evangelist was given a much better hearing. Three days later, on the last night of Moody's mission, 52 Cambridge undergraduates went forward to Moody's inquiry area. One of those who went forward was Gerald Lander.

American football player and coach

At the beginning of 1959 Tom Landry was invited to attend
a strange kind of breakfast, at which the Bible would be
studied. Landry thought that he didn't need any more religion
as he already went to church and lived a decent moral upright
life. However, because he could not think of a good enough
reason to deline the invitation, he went along.

Landry was rather taken aback by what he found. For the
first time in his life he found that he was among a group of
people who took the Bible seriously and who seemed to
believe that every word it said was true. Because of his own
scientific training he found himself to be most sceptical
about anything that smacked of miracle and of the spiritual
world in general. But that did not stop him having a strange
experience. He found that the following two Bible passages
from the Sermon on the Mount had a special message for his
soul:

> "Therefore I tell you, do not worry about your life, what you will
> eat or drink; or about your body, what you will wear. Is not life
> more important than food, and the body more important than
> clothes? Look at the birds of the air; they do not sow or reap or
> store away in barns, and yet your heavenly Father feeds them.
> Are you not much more valuable then they? Who of you by wor-
> rying can add a single hour to his life?
>
> "And why do you worry about clothes? See how the lilies of
> the field grow. They do not labour or spin. Yet I tell you that not
> even Solomon in all his splendour was dressed like one of these.
> If that is how God clothes the grass of the field, which is here
> today and tomorrow is thrown into the fire, will he not much
> more clothe you, O you of little faith? So do not worry, saying,
> 'What shall we eat?' or 'What shall we drink?' or 'What shall we
> wear?' For the pagans run after all these things, and your
> heavenly Father knows that you need them. But seek first his
> kingdom and his righteousness, and all these things will be given
> to you as well. Therefore do not worry about tomorrow, for
> tomorrow will worry about itself. Each day has enough trouble
> of its own . . .

"Therefore everyone who hears these words of mine and puts them into practice is like a wise man who built his house on the rock. The rain came down, the streams rose, and the winds blew and beat against that house; yet it did not fall, because it had its foundation on the rock. But everyone who hears these words of mine and does not put them into practice is like a foolish man who built his house on sand. The rain came down, the streams rose, and the winds blew and beat against that house, and it fell with a great crash."

(Matthew 6:25–34; 7:24–27)

Even though Landry had recently enjoyed such great success as a professional American football player with the New York Yankees and the New York Giants, he found that he did not feel fulfilled by the life he was living. So he wondered at this time what it would take to achieve the next goal in life and live life on a higher level. He kept returning to the Bible study breakfasts and especially to the central New Testament teachings.

In his autobiography he writes about what he found during these studied: that we have all sinned and our failure stands between us and God (as Paul writes in Romans 3:23), and that God sent Jesus to take the punishment for our failure (as John writes in John 3:16). From Paul's letter to the Romans he learned that God's salvation is a free gift for anyone who accepts it. We can do nothing to earn it, we just have to believe. He saw that God wants us to turn our lives over to Him and let Him direct us and provide for all our needs.

Landry had always reckoned that his standing before God was reasonable, as he had attended church all his life. Now he was finding that the teaching of the Bible said that he was just like any other sinner in the world. He realized that doing good things was no substitute for real faith. At this point, he nearly stopped going to those Bible study breakfasts.

Eventually Landry found himself so attracted to the person of Jesus Christ that he was prepared to own up to his own sinfulness, and he gave his life to Christ. Landry's conversion was a fairly cool and calculated one, but it did produce one instantaneous change. His priorities changed from being football first and family last, to God first, family second and football last.

BERNHARD LANGER
German professional golfer
Altar-boy

Bernhard was an altar-boy for some time whilst at school near Augsburg in Germany. He says, "I have always believed in God and always had a certain amount of faith." In 1980 Langer's golfing career reached a significant turning point when he won the Caharel Under-25s tournament. He says that at this time in his life he felt that he was in "nowhere-land".

When Langer played golf in America he found himself going regularly to Bible studies organized by Larry Moody. They made Langer think. He was particularly helped by the example of Scott Simpson, who was to win the 1987 US Open. Simpson battled through a number of personal difficulties before he committed himself to Christ. Langer did the same. He changed his priorities and God became the most important factor in his life.

CHARLES LANHAM
Tail gunner in Lancaster bombers
Isaiah 1:18

At a servicemen's club, a welfare officer asked Lanham why he was so miserable. He also *told* him why he was so miserable: "You are out of touch with God."

A few days later, Lanham told the welfare officer that the Gospel was no use because "I am beyond redemption." The officer denied this and showed him the verse in Isaiah which says:

"'Come now, let us reason together,'
    says the LORD.
'Though your sins are like scarlet,
    they shall be as white as snow;

139

> though they are red as crimson,
> they shall be like wool'" (Isaiah 1:18).

Soon Lanham had accepted God's forgiveness and was a changed man.

R. G. LeTOURNEAU
World's leading manufacturer of
earth-moving equipment

16 years old

LeTourneau was brought up in a Christian family by parents who sincerely loved the Lord Jesus Christ and who encouraged their children to love Him too. By the age of 16 LeTourneau had turned his back on all of this and was quietly going his own way. But he began to realize that there was something going wrong in his life. He knew all about salvation. He had memorised many Bible verses with his family. He had attended countless revival meetings which had helped him, but only for a short time.

Four evenings in succession he went to a revival campaign. Then he stayed at home the fifth night to think things over. On the last night of the campaign he went again but did not go forward at the end of the service. That night at home he thought of the seriousness of being accountable to God and how dreadful it would be to be judged by God. In his heart he cried out, "Lord, save me or else I will perish!" From that moment he knew that he had the gift of eternal salvation from Jesus Christ.

C. S. LEWIS
Literary historian,
popular theologian and writer

On the way
to Whipsnade Zoo

C. S. Lewis was alone in his room at Magdalen College, Oxford, when he found that his thoughts kept returning to the subject of God, whom, he says, he did not want to meet. He gave in to God in 1929 when he knelt down and acknowledged that God was indeed God. He felt as if he was "the most dejected and reluctant convert in all England".

At this stage Lewis thought of God as being other than human, and he did not think about Jesus Christ being God incarnate.

As he saw the truth of Jesus being man as well as God, he again put up great resistance, just as he had before he was prepared to admit that God was God.

This final step in Lewis' Christian conversion took place while he travelled on a bus to visit Whipsnade Zoo. It was a lovely sunny morning. When he left Oxford he did not believe that Jesus Christ was the Son of God. By the time that he arrived at Whipsnade he did believe that Jesus Christ was the Son of God. Yet Lewis recalls that he had not spent the journey deep in thought. He did not have any great emotional feelings linked to this change of heart. Lewis says that some people are very unemotional about some of the most important events in their lives. He likened his conversion experience to being like a man who, after a long sleep, still lies motionless in bed, and who gradually becomes aware that he is awake.

ABRAHAM LINCOLN   *In tragedy*
19th-century President of the United States

Although Abraham Lincoln is often thought of as being America's most Christian President, it appears that he did not come to have a personal relationship with Jesus Christ until towards the end of his time in office.

Lincoln's youngest child, Willie, suddenly died and the President could find no consolation in his personal grief. At this time the nurse who had been caring for Willie shared with the President her own faith in the Lord Jesus Christ and even went so far as to encourage the President to put his trust in her Saviour. Lincoln admits that he did not do this at the time, but later he speaks about a new peace he discovered in his life. He says that when he went to Willie's funeral he was not a Christian. He found Willie's death the greatest trial in his life. But Lincoln says that when he went to see all the graves at Gettysburg, he gave his life to Christ. He wrote, "I then and there consecrated myself to Christ."

GRAHAM LLOYD-DAVIES *In a Welsh chapel*
British Rugby Union player

Graham Lloyd-Davies made a conscious decision not to be religious, even though his parents were well known for their support of the local Welsh chapel. But when a close friend of his, Susan, died in a car crash during his days as a lower sixth former, Graham found himself thinking about God as he carried Susan's coffin at the funeral.

In order to say goodbye to people just before setting out on a rugby tour, Graham went to the chapel. That night the preacher spoke about Jesus Christ being the world's Saviour. At the end of the service he challenged people to come to the front of the chapel so that they could commit themselves to Jesus Christ. To the surprise of those present, Graham, with his younger brother Adrian, went to the front of the chapel. They now knew for themselves that Jesus Christ had died for their sins and was alive today to be with them.

NOEL LOBAN *"Mind-readers"*
American weightlifter

During his first year at college Noel Loban met an American football player called Rocky. Rocky lived like a Christian and did not just call himself a Christian. At this stage Noel did not know that there was any distinction between calling yourself a Christian and becoming a Christian.

Noel started going to the Bible studies which Rocky held. He found that the discussions always spoke to his heart. He thought that the people must be mind-readers, as the discussions applied to him personally each time. Then Noel read the Bible for himself. He committed his life to Jesus Christ. He gave up drugs and quickly earned the nickname of "religious Joe". About a year after this Noel became a member of Rocky's football team.

DENIS LOCKWOOD   *A film in prison*
Ex-offender

Seventy cigarettes a day and a bottle of rum in fifteen minutes – that was Denis Lockwood when he was still in the army just after World War II. He'd met and married an Austrian girl while posted abroad, and was idyllically happy, but she and their baby had died in childbirth and Denis had collapsed into drinking and gambling.

Civilian life held no attraction for him after his demobilization – he didn't want to work, and his family were of no help. For a few years he drifted, and lived by embezzling money; then the police caught up with him and he landed in prison.

A Billy Graham film was shown in the prison one day, and that was the means of Denis' conversion. The words of the hymn 'Softly and tenderly' kept going through his mind, and back in his prison cell he prayed, accepting Jesus as his Saviour, because he felt he had found an answer to his problems, and one that would work.

It worked for him because, he says, "not only has He forgiven all my sins but He has changed me completely ... He helps me overcome all temptations to return to my old way of life and gives me peace and joy in His love."

MARTIN LUTHER
16th-century German theologian

God as parent

Luther sought to do penance for his sins as he was training to be a monk. He went without food, drink and sleep. He beat himself until he drew blood. One day, when he had been missing for some time, two monks tapped on his cell door. Getting no answer, they entered to find him unconscious on the floor, his thin body covered with blood.

When Luther visited Rome he saw the Scala Sancta, the 28 sacred steps which Jesus mounted to meet Pontius Pilate. Luther was overawed. Believing that, with every step he climbed, a soul would be released from Purgatory, he went on all fours, stopping to pray at each step for his dead brothers, grandparents and other deceased relatives. Now that he could release their sinful souls from torment, he even half wished his parents were dead. Then, at the top, he turned, looked down the stairs and asked himself, "Is it true?"

After Luther had received his doctorate he engaged in teaching, at which he was brilliant. He made everything simple so that students could grasp the most difficult Bible passages, and his lectures were the best attended in the university. And as he taught, Luther was slowly learning the answers to all his own questions. The letters of Paul showed that God loved sinners as much as saints. His love and forgiveness could not be won or earned. God did not look for perfection but loved mankind despite its human frailties, and when Jesus Christ died on the cross, His suffering was for their sins. Luther suddenly saw God, not as a stern judge eager to punish all wrongdoers, but as the parent who loves the naughty child as much as the good one. So Luther found inner peace from God for himself.

JANANI LUWUM
"Jesus overwhelmed me"
Archbishop of Uganda, martyred under Idi Amin

Though born into a Christian home, Janani Luwum was not himself converted until he was 26. Two of the people who had been converted in the East African revival of the 1930s came to lead a mission in his home village, and Janani was converted along with his brother and six other members of his family.

"Today I have become a leader in Christ's army," he declared when he was converted. He was so awed and joyful because of the peace he felt on account of Christ's death and resurrection for his forgiveness, that he climbed a tree to tell people to repent and turn to Jesus. "The reality of Jesus overwhelmed me," he said later, "and it still does."

LYDIA
Speaking to the women
1st-century cloth merchant in Philippi

From Troas we put out to sea and sailed straight for Samothrace, and the next day on to Neapolis. From there we travelled to Philippi, a Roman colony and the leading city of that district of Macedonia. And we stayed there several days.

On the Sabbath we went outside the city gate to the river, where we expected to find a place of prayer. We sat down and began to speak to the women who had gathered there. One of those listening was a woman named Lydia, a dealer in purple cloth from the city of Thyatira, who was a worshipper of God. The Lord opened her heart to respond to Paul's message. When she and the members of her household were baptised, she invited us to her home. "If you consider me a believer in the Lord," she said, "come and stay at my house." And she persuaded us.

Acts 16:11–15

HENRY FRANCIS LYTE
19th-century hymn-writer

Lyte gained the prize for the English Poem three times at Trinity College, Dublin. His first curacy was near Wexford, but in 1817 he moved to Marazion, Cornwall. There he formed a friendship with a neighbouring clergyman. His friend had not found peace in Christ. He and Lyte, who were not yet awake to spiritual realities, searched the Bible together, and learnt the way of salvation. Lyte's friend died soon afterwards, in 1818. Lyte wrote: "He died happy, under the belief that though he had deeply erred, there was One whose death and sufferings would atone for his delinquencies, and be accepted for all that he had incurred. I began to study my Bible, and preach in another manner than I had previously done."

JERRY McAULEY
Founder of the Water Street Mission in New York

Jerry McAuley was sentenced to prison for 16½ years. He was 19. One day the preacher in chapel was "Awful Gardiner" – a prize-fighter and thug whom Jerry had known outside. There were tears streaming down Gardiner's face as he told about Jesus' love. Gardiner quoted the Bible, and afterwards Jerry found a Bible in his cell. He had never held one before, and found it hard to read but, whilst trying to find the verse Gardiner had quoted, he read that Jesus had died for sinners – and the Holy Spirit showed him that he was a sinner.

"I've found Jesus," he shouted. "Oh, bless the Lord, I've found Jesus." The noise drew the attention of the warder, who shouted, "What's the matter with you?"

"I've found Jesus," replied Jerry.

"I'll put you in the cooler in the morning," the warder said, and took down his number.

"The Lord made him forget it, for I was never put in the

cooler," said Jerry later.

Revival came to the prison. Missionaries from the city visited, and Jerry was the centre of activity. He was pardoned by the State Governor, eight years of his sentence being remitted.

STEVE McQUEEN
American actor
Dying of cancer

Steve tried to hide his illness from the world. He went to live with his wife in a very isolated ranch and visitors were banned. Slowly, people began to talk about Steve's cancer. He eventually went into hospital and a 2½-pound tumour was removed from his abdomen. He survived the operation only to succumb to a massive fatal heart attack 24 hours later.

A little-known fact is that a few weeks before this Steve asked a visitor to his hideout. Billy Graham made a special trip by plane and jeep to Steve's ranch. During their conversation Steve committed his life to the Lord Jesus Christ. It was the most momentous event of his exciting life. As Billy Graham made to leave, Steve asked a favour of the famous evangelist. Steve asked Billy for his Bible. Billy gladly gave it to Steve with a suitable inscription hastily written on the flyleaf. Billy Graham's Bible reminded Steve about the day of his conversion and about the presence of the living Christ whom he trusted during the last days of his illness. Steve read this Bible, took it into hospital with him and treasured it.

MARTIN MADAN
18th-century English clergyman
Taken off

In 1748 a young barrister was enjoying the company of his friends at a coffee-house. He must have been well regarded as a mimic, because his friends asked him to go and hear John

Wesley, who was preaching close by, and then come back and do an impersonation of him. Off went Madan, and he got to the church in time to hear Wesley announce the text of his sermon in very sombre tones: "Prepare to meet thy God."

Madan found himself listening, not just to pick up the preacher's mannerisms, but in earnest. The sermon was a call to repentance. When he reappeared in the coffee-house his friends asked him, "Well, have you taken off the old Methodist?" and were astonished to hear his utterly sober reply, "No, gentlemen, but he has taken me off." That was the end of Madan's association with that group of friends; he now worked to become a minister himself.

Madan became a hospital chaplain in 1750, and the chapel of the hospital in which he worked remained a conspicuous evangelical beacon in London for the next 30 years.

GEOFF MANN   *"When I knew Christ died for me"*
Musician, singer and Christian minister

Geoff Mann heard God talk to him in 1980. He was told that Christ had died for him. Geoff found that this message was exactly what he needed to know then. It answered all the questions he had in his mind about the meaning of life. He quickly realized that he was not mulling over some abstract thought that he did not have to react to. He knew that his knowledge that Christ died for him demanded that he make a response to the person of Christ. And this Geoff did at that moment in 1980.

CATHERINE MARSHALL   *A blank cheque*
American writer and widow
of preacher Peter Marshall

While in bed one morning Catherine Marshall read the parable recorded in Matthew 12:43–45:

"When an evil spirit comes out of a man, it goes through arid places seeking rest and does not find it. Then it says, 'I will return to the house I left.' When it arrives, it finds the house unoccupied, swept clean and put in order. Then it goes and takes with it seven other spirits more wicked than itself, and they go in and live there. And the final condition of that man is worse than the first. That is how it will be with this wicked generation."

Catherine knew that she had to let Christ take over and run her life.

So on that bright sunny June morning Catherine got out of bed and made her momentous decision. She pledged herself to God. It was like writing out a blank cheque with her life.

This happened at 10.12 a.m. on 22nd June 1944. She promised God that she would do whatever He told her to do for the rest of her life.

HENRY MARTYN
Missionary in India
A living Person

Henry Martyn received countless first prizes for his hard work and brilliance at St John's College, Cambridge. But he found that these human accolades did not satisfy him. He was persuaded to start reading the Bible by a friend and by his younger sister. Shortly after this Jesus Christ, rather than his studies, became the centre of his life.

Remembering this time in his life, Martyn wrote, "Soon I began to attend more diligently to the words of our Saviour in the New Testament, and to devour them with delight." When he realized that Christ was offering to forgive him he responded wholeheartedly and prayed for his own salvation. His discovery was not some theological doctrine but the Person of our Lord Jesus Christ. This was Martyn's conversion.

It was high commendation, and the like seldom known, that
[he] should be found fit to teach and govern a school at fifteen years of age: and yet the Lord helped him in those his
young years to carry it with such wisdom, love, and gravity
among his scholars, as was to admiration ...

There the more effectual conversion of his soul unto the
Lord was wrought in his tender years, even before his going
to the University of Oxford ...

The means of his conversion was partly by observing a
strange difference between himself and sundry in that godly
family of Mr Edward Aspinwal ... a learned and religious
gentleman; and Mr Mather took notice of the way and walking of that holy man, which was such as himself had not yet
been accustomed unto, which caused sad fears to rise in his
soul, lest haply he might not be in the right way which leads
unto eternal life: also Mr Harrison ... preaching upon John
3:3 concerning the necessity of regeneration, and Mr Mather
at the same time reading a book published by William
Perkins ...

The pangs of the new birth were very terrible to him,
insomuch as many times when others were at their meals in
the family where he sojourned, he oft absented himself, to
retire under hedges, and in other secret places, there to lament
his misery before God: but after some time, the Lord revived
his broken heart, by sending the Holy Spirit to accompany
the ministry of the word, and to enable him to apply the
precious promises of the gospel to his soul.

Being thus become a new creature, he was more eminently
a blessing in that family, and in that calling which the Lord
had disposed him in ...

The Lives of Sundry Eminent Persons in this Later Age, Samuel Clarke,
Simmons, 1683, pp. 127–128

MAU MAU TERRORIST   *Revelation 21:7–8*
Kenyan hotel manager, formerly a terrorist

When Kenya was struggling for independence in the 1950s, Mau Mau terrorists were going about murdering people, and especially those who were professing Christians. One such terrorist, while he was being held in a detention camp, listened to a sermon by an African Christian minister on Revelation 21:7–8: "He who overcomes will inherit all this, and I will be his God, and he will be my son. But the cowardly, the unbelieving, the vile, the murderers, the sexually immoral, those who practise magic arts, the idolaters and all liars – their place will be in the fiery lake of burning sulphur. This is the second death."

For some days the young man reflected on these verses, and on his own sin, and then one night he prayed, seeking Jesus' saving power. A few days later he dreamed that a man was about to kill him with a sword; he called out Jesus' name, and woke to find that his cry had been real and had been heard by some of his fellow prisoners. After this experience, he became assured that he was saved from sin.

"His blood worked very hard in my heart," he wrote. "Since then I never feel tired of my sins as all were taken in the West and I was left in the East, and now there is a very big river between me and where those sins are."

HUSSEIN MEMOUR   *Arab evangelist*
Turkish Cypriot converted from Islam

At an American boarding school in Cyprus, Hussein Memour found himself forced to live alongside students of other nationalities – even Greeks, Armenians and others he regarded as enemies.

He began to learn basic facts about the Bible and about Christianity; and he went to a meeting in the school chapel at which the guest speaker was an Arab from Egypt, who had become a Christian. This evangelist told how he had picked up a Gospel and been converted through his reading of it.

It impressed Memour that this speaker seemed able to put up with persecution and even to rejoice under it. So the ground was prepared for the reception of the evangelist's key verse: "For God so loved the world that he gave his one and only Son, that whoever believes in him shall not perish but have eternal life" (John 3:16). Memour accepted its message for himself that night, and took a firm stand for Jesus at the school. Later he carefully talked to his parents and sisters about his new-found faith, and they allowed him to travel to Paris and later to London, to study for full-time Christian work.

GEORGE MENSIK   *Four years*
Chicago gangster

Mensik's wife was converted through a radio programme. He waited for her 'religion' to wear off, but it didn't; she didn't talk much about it, but simply prayed a lot for him. After four years he decided he'd have to go to her church to get ammunition to use against her religion. He went to two services, and was converted. He learned that what he had seen his wife acquire was not "religion" but new life.

As a Christian, he gave up the gangs, got a mundane job and told people about Jesus. Needing a gun permit in order to take a job as a security guard, he went to see the police commissioner – and brought with him half a dozen people who testified to his change of character. The commissioner was so impressed that he tore up Mensik's criminal record.

"No religion could have kept my wife through the stormy four years," he wrote later, "and no religion could have brought me out of the mobs and given me a clean sheet. Only Christ could do that."

JOHN METCALFE
Evangelist

Frittering away his money on drink, as his father had done before him, John Metcalfe found his life so bleak that he very nearly committed suicide. He was in the Navy, and actually climbed over the bows of his ship and hung above the waters beneath; but something (God? he wondered) stopped him letting go, and he made a vague vow to serve God.

When he got back home he found that his mother, grandmother and stepfather had all become Christians, though when they talked about their faith he found it difficult to understand. His mother persuaded him to attend a series of evangelistic meetings, and he talked with the speaker about his need. He struggled against accepting Christ, but the speaker stayed with him until the early hours of the morning, praying with him, and finally John found the peace that he had been seeking.

MICHELLE
Convert from Judaism

Born a Jew, Michelle came to admire Christian students at the University of Cape Town, where she was studying maths. She joined a Christian houseparty, where she herself met Jesus.

For her, the keynote was joy. A friend to whom she was describing her experience on the telephone told her how clearly the joy could be heard in her voice, and Michelle learned that this was not a purely temporary emotion. To begin with, she was apprehensive about telling her Jewish friends that she was now a Christian, but later she found that she wanted everybody to know. She was following in the way her Lord wanted her to go, and she was full of a deep-seated contentment to be doing so.

CHARLES MIDDLETON, LORD BARHAM
A sweetheart's prayers

First Lord of the Admiralty at the time of Trafalgar

Charles Middleton was in love. But the girl he loved, who truly loved him in return, would not marry him. She was a Christian, and she was simply not prepared to marry someone who did not himself trust her Lord. She knew such a marriage would not work.

Because she loved the young naval lieutenant, however, she prayed for him, and took him to hear the great evangelist George Whitefield. Charles was indeed brought to personal faith, which opened the way for their marriage – a marriage which was to give the couple great happiness until Margaret's sudden death in 1792.

Middleton rose to become Comptroller of the Navy, in which capacity he faced the corruption that was rife in naval administration and introduced Christian moral values to the service. And when the First Lord of the Admiralty was forced out of office in 1805, it was Middleton whom the Prime Minister appointed in his place, as Lord Barham, to plan the last few months of the war with France. Everything he did was undertaken in the power of prayer, as he committed each event to God.

D. L. MOODY
In a shoe store

American evangelist

D. L. Moody is credited with being the first mass evangelist in modern times and it has been estimated that over 100 million people heard or read the Gospel message as a result of this one man.

At 17 Moody was a shoe salesman working for his uncle Sam Holton. At his uncle's insistence Moody attended the Vernon Congregational Church in Boston. In that church Moody listened with rapt attention to the fiery sermons of the church's pastor, Edwark Kirk. There he saw in front of his eyes hardened sinners being melted by the love of God.

But it wasn't a sermon in a crowded church that brought the future evangelist to Christ. It was the caring, faithful words of his Sunday school teacher. Edward Kimball visited Moody in his shoe shop and found him out at the back packing up shoes. Kimball looked Moody straight in the eye and asked him if he would come to Christ. Kimball explained to Moody that Christ loved him and that Christ deserved to be loved by Moody in return. So Moody committed his life to Christ.

LOTTIE MOON *A barking dog*
American missionary to China

This remarkable woman said in her later life that if she had a thousand lives she would give them all for the women of China, where she had become a dedicated missionary.

She dates her conversion precisely. It happened three days before Christmas Day in 1858. She had attended an evangelistic meeting held by Dr John Broadus at Charlottesville Baptist Church and was deeply moved by his address. Lottie went to bed but was unable to sleep because a barking dog kept her awake. So through the night she thought about the truths of Christianity and the claims which Christ had on her life. In the small hours of the morning she committed her life to Christ.

HANNAH MORE *Progressive renewal*
Author of religious books and
pioneer of Sunday Schools

Hannah More strongly disliked the word "conversion" – calling it obnoxious. In her book *Practical Piety* she described conversion as a continuous process in the life of the believer. He or she sees the evils of the world and moves forward to a life of "progressive piety", showing by changes in conduct the changes that have taken place in the heart.

Hannah became, in the words of one biographer, "obedient to the law of God, converting the soul and giving light to the eyes, so that she was transformed by the renewing of her mind".

HANDLEY MOULE
19th-century scholar, preacher and Bishop of Durham

Conviction of sin

Although he was a successful schoolmaster and scholar, Handley Moule was inwardly discontented. "A profound conviction of the fatal guilt of sin, the sin of resistance of the will to the blessed Maker and Master of my being, found its way to my heart. That dark time ended in a full and conscious acceptance of our crucified Redeemer, Christ our Sacrifice in His complete atonement as peace and life," he wrote later.

After retreating during the school holidays to a remote part of Scotland, he wrote to his father, a parson: "My trust is that I was able to find and accept pardon and peace and to feel a truth and solid reality in the doctrine of the Cross as I have ever been taught it at home, such as I had sometimes very painfully doubted of, under the continual droppings of the controversies and questions of the present day."

GEORGE MÜLLER
Man of prayer and founder of orphanages

Kneeling

A Saturday evening at Mr Wagner's house was the turning point in George Müller's history and destiny. He found himself in strange company, amid novel surroundings. All present sat down and sang a hymn. Then a brother fell on his knees and prayed for God's blessing on

156

the meeting. That kneeling before God in prayer made upon Müller an impression never lost. He was in his twenty-first year, and yet he had never before seen anyone on his knees praying, and of course had never himself knelt before God – the Prussian habit being to stand in public prayer.

A chapter was read from the word of God and a printed sermon was read. When, after another hymn, the master of the house prayed, George Müller was inwardly saying: "I am much more learned than this illiterate man, but I could not pray as well as he." Strange to say, a new joy was already springing up in his soul for which he could have given as little explanation as for his unaccountable desire to go to that meeting. But so it was; and on the way home he could not forbear saying to Beta: "All we saw on our journey to Switzerland, and all our former pleasures, are as nothing compared to this evening."

Whether or not, on reaching his own room, he himself knelt to pray he could not recall, but he never forgot that a new and strange peace and rest somehow found him as he lay in bed that night ...

George Müller's eyes were but half opened, as though he saw men as trees walking; but Christ had touched those eyes. He knew little of the great Healer, but somehow he had touched the hem of His garment of grace, and virtue came out of Him who wears that seamless robe, and who responds even to the faintest contact of the soul that is groping after salvation. That Saturday evening in November, 1825, was to this young student of Halle the parting of the ways. He had tasted that the Lord is gracious.

George Müller of Bristol, A. T. Pierson, 1899

JIMMY MURPHY   *No hoper*
Reformed young offender

An unhappy childhood in London's East End led Jimmy
Murphy into a teenage life of burglary, rioting and drugs.
God seemed an irrelevance, and the boy's mother told a
curate there was no hope for Jimmy.

But God held out hope for him. That same curate set up a
youth club for lads like Jimmy, and told them that God could
help them if they'd only give Him a chance. "Your heavenly
Father is only a prayer away," he said.

In time, Jimmy did pray, confessing that nothing he tried
to do worked out right, and asking God to come into his life
and change him. There weren't any immediately obvious
signs of change, but Jimmy now thinks that he was like a
caterpillar changing into a butterfly: there had to be a
chrysalis stage. In retrospect, he is amazed at what has taken
place since then.

ANDREW MURRAY   *Surrender*
19th-century South African evangelist

Students who leave the paternal roof to study abroad frequently sever their moorings and find themselves adrift upon
sunless seas of doubt. Others, again, who have been reared
in piety and nurtured on Bible truth, when thrown upon
their own spiritual resources, find occasion amid the uncon-
genial surroundings for committing themselves anew to the
grace of an all-sufficient Saviour. Thus it befell with Andrew
Murray.

At Utrecht he underwent the great change which he called
his conversion, and which made him more definitely the
Lord's. He used to say that he could point to the very house,
the very room, and of course the very date, when this change
ensued. His conversion was no sudden upheaval, but it was a
distinct and complete surrender to Christ and to His claims —
a clear-cut experience from which he dated a new era, and

which lay at the back of all the preaching of later years. The news of this event was conveyed to his parents in the following letter:

... When I look back to see how I have been brought to where I now am, I must acknowledge that I see nothing. "He hath brought the blind by a way that he knew not, and led him in a path that he hath not known." For the last two or three years there has been a process going on, a continual interchange of seasons of seriousness and then of forgetfulness, and then again of seriousness soon after. In this state I came here, and as you may well conceive there was little seriousness amid the bustle of coming away. After leaving [Scotland], however, there was an interval of seriousness during the three days we were at sea – our departure from Aberdeen, the sea, recollections of the past, all were calculated to lead one to reflect. But after I came to Holland I think I was led to pray in earnest: more I cannot tell, for I know it not. "Whereas I was blind, now I see." I was long troubled with the idea that I must have some deep sight of my sins before I could be converted, and though I cannot yet say that I have had anything of that deep special sight into the guiltiness of sin which many people appear to have, yet I trust, and at present I feel as if I could say, I am confident that as a sinner I have been led to cast myself on Christ.

The Life of Andrew Murray, J. Du Plessis, Marshall Morgan & Scott, 1919, pp. 63–65

HERMAN NEWMARK   *A borrowed Bible*
Oil company executive and missionary among Jews

Though Jewish by birth, Herman Newmark was an atheist and looked for inspiration to the "brotherhood of man" – which was a rather shaken idea when World War 1 broke out.

He tried to find brotherhood through a Masonic Lodge, but was rather put off by the suspicion that being treated as a Masonic brother could depend on the state of your health and your bank balance.

It seemed sensible to stop ignoring the Creator of mankind, so Herman borrowed a Bible from his landlady (he was working in Japan at the time) and read through the Old

Testament. It impressed him as being self-evidently God's Word. He went on to the New Testament, and found it displayed the same divine character as the Old. It showed the personality of Jesus Christ; it recorded and explained what He had done.

Quite simply, Herman Newmark accepted what the New Testament said about Jesus bearing the penalty for man's sin, and began to pray. In forgiveness he found new life, which he started to share, first with his Japanese neighbours and later with his own people in London.

JOHN NEWTON
Great Deliverance
18th-century English clergyman and hymn-writer, formerly a slave trader

On his way home in 1748 Newton spent a night on a water-logged boat, with death staring him in the face, but found that this was the moment when God spoke to his conscience.

Later Newton referred to this time as the "Great Deliverance":

I went to bed that night in my usual security and indifference; but was awakened from a sound sleep by the force of a violent sea, which broke on board us. The sea had torn away the upper timbers on one side, and made the ship a mere wreck in a few minutes. Taking in all the circumstances, it was astonishing, and almost miraculous, that any of us survived to relate the story. We had immediate recourse to the pumps; but the water increased against all our efforts: some of us were set to bailing in another part of the vessel, that is, to lade it out with buckets and pails. I continued doing this till noon, with almost every passing wave breaking over my head; but we made ourselves fast with ropes, that we might not be washed away. Although I dreaded death now, I thought, if the Christian religion was true, I could not be forgiven.

The next day I began to pray. My prayer was like the cry of the ravens, which yet the Lord does not disdain to hear. I now began to think of that Jesus whom I had so often derided: I recollected the particulars of his life, and of his death; a death for sins not his own, but, as I remembered, for the sake of those who in their distress should put their trust in him. My companions in danger were either quite unaffected, or soon forgot it all: but it was not so with me; not that I was any wiser or better than they, but because the Lord was pleased to vouchsafe me peculiar mercy. I had a New Testament and was struck particularly by the Prodigal, Luke chapter 15. Before we arrived in Ireland I had a satisfactory evidence in my own mind of the truth of the Gospel, as considered in itself, and its exact suitableness to answer all my needs. I saw that, by the way there pointed out, God might declare, not his mercy only, but his justice also, in the pardon of sin, on the account of the obedience and sufferings of Jesus Christ. My judgement at that time embraced the sublime doctrine of "God manifest in the flesh, reconciling the world to himself."

Collected Letters, John Newton, edited by Halcyon Backhouse, Hodder & Stoughton, 1989, pp. 8–9

RITA NIGHTINGALE   *In a Thai jail*
Imprisoned in the Far East on a drugs charge

Rita was in prison awaiting notice of the length of her prison sentence, as she had been found guilty of attempting to smuggle 3.3 kilos of heroin at Bangkok airport. She reached into her bag for a tissue and found a Christian booklet called *The Reason Why.*

As Rita read it she felt as if every word had been especially written for her. Yes, she had been the victim of the wickedness of others. Rita was beside herself wondering why she was imprisoned so unjustly and why her family had to suffer so much as a result. As she continued to read the booklet she agreed with what it said. Yes, everybody was selfish. Nobody was naturally good. Yes, she was angry with God. Yes, she was bitter about being treated so badly by life.

Rita then saw from this booklet that all this sadness in the world is what the Bible calls sin. And because of sin people are not able to have the necessary link with God they need, because He is pure and holy. Then Rita suddenly saw her own selfishness and hardness.

Then Rita read how God had acted. He had taken the initiative to solve mankind's problem. He had sent Jesus

Christ on a rescue mission. Christ died for the human race and then came back to life again.

Rita could now make sense of everything that happened in the world. Suddenly there was an explanation for everything. She was also acutely aware that God was not in her life as He ought to be. Rita prayed about the mess she had made of her life. She told God she was sorry for not wanting Him and then asked Him into her life.

Rita then knew for herself that God had created her, that God knew her and that Jesus Christ loved her.

DEREK NIMMO
British actor
Beach mission

A holiday beach mission led Derek Nimmo as a child to find fun in Christianity. As a result of that mission he committed his life to Jesus Christ, with a great sense of the importance of his action.

As he moved from school to college, he went through a period of unbelief, but returned to his faith through reading and reflection at a monastery in Cyprus. He then felt "enormous relief at the sheer simplicity of it, and a great sense of purpose in life".

BROWNLOW NORTH
Scottish lay preacher
James 4:2–4

Extravagant to the point where his uncle, the Earl of Guildford, disinherited him, Brownlow North's chief delights were drinking, gambling and grouse-shooting. A Christian lady told him, in the words of James 4:2–4: "Ye lust, and have not: ye kill, and desire to have, and cannot obtain: ye fight and war, yet ye have not, because ye ask not. Ye ask, and receive not, because ye ask amiss, that ye may consume it upon your lusts. Ye adulterers and adulteresses, know ye not that the friendship of the world is enmity with God? Whosoever therefore will be a friend of the world is the enemy of God."

He changed his ways, read for ordination, and yet was spiritually empty. The bishop would not ordain him and he reverted to his former ways.

When he was 44, he had a sudden heart attack and thought he was going to die. In fear, rather than conviction, he prayed, but then he knew this was the moment – his last chance – when he must change. The following day, when he announced that he had given his heart to Christ, "he seemed as if just risen from a long illness, and very gentle and subdued in manner". After a further six months he knew the truth of Paul's letter to the Romans, that Christ had done everything and all he needed to do was to trust Him.

Later, when he was visiting London, he heard a young man preaching in the streets near King's Cross. The man was boring the rough crowd, who were telling him so in no uncertain terms; but one of the listeners said, "We'll hear that stout man with the dark eyes," and Brownlow North found himself not only preaching, but holding the crowd's attention amazingly. He knew his sins, and knew God's mercy in receiving him.

THOMAS OLIVERS   *Delinquent*
18th-century Welsh Methodist preacher and hymn-writer

Thomas Olivers, born in Montgomeryshire in 1725, was orphaned before he was five. The people he grew up with often lied and swore, and by the time Thomas was 15 he was the worst boy known in the district for 20 or 30 years. He was apprenticed to a shoemaker, but he had to leave the neighbourhood because of his behaviour.

He went to Bristol, where he heard a sermon preached by George Whitefield and was convicted of sin. He fasted and prayed till his knees grew stiff. "So earnest was I that I used by the hour together to wrestle with all the might of my body and soul, till I almost expected to die on the spot," he said.

YOHANA OMARI
**Bishop of Ukaguru and Unguu in
Tanganyika (now Tanzania)**

John 14:6

Omari came from a Muslim family but was sent to Christian mission schools. From school he stole a New Testament in Swahili, and while looking through it he came across the words: "Jesus answered, 'I am the way and the truth and the life. No-one comes to the Father except through me.'" If Christ was the only way to God, reasoned Omari, then Muhammad could not also be the way. The Bible seemed to have a ring of truth, so the Qur'ān could not also be true.

From that beginning Omari went on along a path that took him to rejecting Islam and accepting Christ; to pioneering missionary work; and to ordination. He was a leading figure in the East African Revival. He learned a special lesson of discipleship:

> Although I performed God's work very hard, I appeared a very poor person in the face of Him. I committed numerous sins; there was no peace in my home and no peace in my soul. It was not until the Lord Jesus revealed all these things to me that I bowed at His cross and confessed all my sins and I believe He delivered me from them. Since then I have continued to entrust my life to Him, and I thank Him for peace in my home and my heart.

LISA OPIE
Women's world squash champion

In Sydney

Lisa Opie had been playing squash in Sydney for four days and staying with her friend Barbara Oldfield during this time. Although Lisa did not know it at the time, Barbara was already praying that she might become a Christian. Lisa went along with Barbara to a church service, throughout which Lisa could not stop perspiring. In tears and great joy she gave her life to the Lord Jesus Christ at the end of the service.

Then the former Wimbledon tennis champion Margaret Court spoke to her and explained how the Lord Jesus Christ had died for her sins and that she was now forgiven.

Lisa now cherishes the following words of the apostle Paul, as she has found out for herself that there is much more to life than being a world squash champion: "Do you not know that in a race all the runners run, but only one gets the prize? Run in such a way as to get the prize. Everyone who competes in the games goes into strict training. They do it to get a crown that will not last; but we do it to get a crown that will last for ever."

NOBUYOSHI OSHIMA
Converted Japanese Buddhist

The Japanese "Gi" character

The ending of World War II brought both relief and doubt to the young Oshima. Relief, because he had been training as a kamikaze pilot and was now released from flying duty. Doubt, because the Emperor's admission that he was not a god undermined all the lad's religious beliefs.

His father, a Zen Buddhist, had taught him that man could be saved through his own efforts. His mother, an Ikko Buddhist, had taught him that salvation came from the Buddha through the repetition of prayers. At school, he had been taught Shinto beliefs.

He found inconsistencies in Marxism, in Soka Gakkai and in Christianity too, though he attended a number of church meetings and even attempted to convert his father to Christianity.

Then he responded to an invitation to an evangelistic meeting, where the speaker said that the Japanese "Gi"

165

character, for "righteousness", meant "me under the Lamb", and that the blood of the Lamb, Jesus, had the power to make people righteous in God's sight.

This brought light to Oshima's darkness and he received Christ. Two years later he was to lead another evangelistic meeting in the same hall, with the same speaker, and to see his wife accept Christ too.

JOHN OWEN
17th-century English theologian

Why fear?

For years Owen had been under the power of religious principle, but he had not yet been borne into the region of settled peace; and at times the terrors of the Lord seemed still to compass him about.

But the time had come when the burden was to fall from Owen's shoulders; and few things in his life are more truly interesting than the means by which it was unloosed. Dr Edmund Calamy was at this time minister in Aldermanbury Chapel, and attracted multitudes by his eloquence. Owen had gone one Sabbath morning to hear the celebrated Presbyterian preacher, and much was disappointed when he saw an unknown stranger from the country enter the pulpit. His companion suggested that they should leave the chapel, and hasten to the place of worship of another celebrated preacher; but Owen's strength being already exhausted, he determined to remain. After a prayer of simple earnestness, the text was announced in these words of Matthew 8:26, "Why are ye fearful, O ye of little faith?" Immediately it arrested the thoughts of Owen as appropriate to his present state of mind, and he breathed an inward prayer that God would be pleased by that minister to speak to his condition. The prayer was heard, for the preacher stated and answered the very doubts that had long perplexed Owen's mind; and by the time that the discourse was ended, had succeeded in leading him forth into the sunshine of a settled peace. The most diligent efforts were used by Owen to discover the name of the preacher who had thus been to him "as an angel of God", but without success.

The Works of John Owen, Vol. 1, Johnstone & Hunter, 1850

J. I. PACKER   *God tracked him down*
British theologian

James Innell Packer entered Oxford University in 1944 and then experienced biblical Christianity for the first time.

In his first term at Oxford, aged 18, he was visited by a fellow student who was a member of the local branch of the Inter-Varsity Christian Fellowship, which in Oxford was known as the Oxford Inter Collegiate Christian Union. In his own way Packer already believed in Jesus Christ, but his belief was no stronger than a mental assent. Packer felt as if he was on the outside of a house where a tremendous happy party was going on. However, God tracked him down and he was surprised by God's grace.

LUIS PALAU   *Torchlight confession*
Argentinian evangelist

Luis Palau's conversion happened at a boy's summer camp. Each night one of the leaders of the camp, a Mr Chandler, would wake up one of the boys and take him outside his tent. In the light of a torch he would then open his Bible and explain how the boy could put his trust in Jesus Christ.

When Luis Palau was tapped on the shoulder he tried to pretend that he was so soundly asleep that he didn't know that Mr Chandler was there. But Mr Chandler persisted and got Luis out of his tent.

Mr Chandler asked Luis if he was a Christian or not and Luis could only reply that he did not think so. Mr Chandler persisted again until Luis agreed that he was not a Christian.

Mr Chandler's next question showed Luis that he meant business that night. If Luis died that night, he was asked, would he go to heaven or hell? Reluctantly, Luis had to admit that he would go to hell.

No, Luis did not want to go to hell and could not think of any reasonable reply to Mr Chandler's next question, which was, why was he going to hell if he didn't really want to?

At this juncture Mr Chandler opened his Bible and read Romans 10:9–10: "If you confess with your lips, Luis, that Jesus is Lord and believe in your heart, Luis, that God raised him from the dead, you, Luis, will be saved. For man believes with his heart and so is justified, and he confesses with his lips and so is saved."

Mr Chandler then continued to question Luis closely. Now he wanted to know if Luis did believe that God brought Jesus back from the dead. Luis was able to reply to this in the affirmative. Then came the crunch question, as he was asked what he must do if he did truly want to be saved.

Luis hesitated so long that Mr Chandler made him read Romans 10:9 for himself this time: "If you confess with your mouth 'Jesus is Lord' ... you will be saved."

Mr Chandler then prayed a prayer with Luis with his arm around him. The twelve-year-old Luis asked Christ into his heart as he sat in the rain on a log next to Mr Chandler. At once he knew the truth of John 10:28, that he had eternal life because Christ said, "I give them eternal life, and they shall never perish; no-one can snatch them out of my hand."

Good conventional Catholics, the Pascals performed their religious duties regularly but with little conviction. When they were introduced to Cyprian's theology, especially his teaching about God's free grace, they moved away from being consumed with material things and devoted themselves to Christ.

On the evening of 23 November 1654 Pascal had a spiritual experience which influenced him him for the rest of his life. He recorded this mystical moment in his *Memorial*, on a scrap of paper, which was later copied onto parchment. This testimony of his conversion was found sown into his clothes after his death. He carried it with him wherever he went.

The Memorial

In the Year of Grace 1654,
On Monday, 23 November, Feast of Saint Clement,
Pope and Martyr,
and of others in the Martyrology,
and Eve of Saint Chrysogonus and other Martyrs,
From about half past ten at night until about half past twelve.

Fire
"God of Abraham, God of Isaac, God of Jacob" (Exodus 6:3),
not of the philosophers and scientists.
Certitude. Certitude. Feeling. Joy. Peace.
God of Jesus Christ.
God of Jesus Christ.

"My God and your God" (John 20:17).

"You shall be my God" (Ruth 1:16).

Forgetting the world and all things, except only God.
He is to be found only by the ways taught in the Gospel.
Greatness of the human soul.

"Righteous Father, the world has not known Thee, but I have

169

known Thee" (John 17:25).

Joy, joy, joy, tears of joy.
I have fallen away from Him.
"They have forsaken me, the fountain of living water"
(Jeremiah 2:13).
"My God, wilt thou forsake me?" (see Matthew 27:46).
May I not be separated from Him in all eternity.
"Now this is eternal life, that they may know Thee, the only true
God, and Jesus Christ, whom Thou hast sent" (John 17:3).

Jesus Christ.
Jesus Christ.
I have fallen away from Him; I have fled from Him, denied Him,
crucified Him.
May I not be separated from Him for eternity.
We hold him only by the ways taught in the Gospel.
Renunciation total and sweet.
Total submission to Jesus Christ and to my director.
Eternally in joy for one day of trial upon earth.
"I will not forget thy Word" (Psalm 119:16). Amen.

COLONEL PASCHKOV   *At a Grand Duchess' soirée*
19th-century darling of
St Petersburg society

Colonel Paschkov, a personal friend of Tsar Alexander II,
was delighted to attend the Grand Duchess' soirée. As he
arrived his attention was drawn to somebody who stood
out in the middle of all this opulence. It was a soberly
dressed Englishman who was speaking in the usual language
of the Russian nobility, French, to a group of fascinated
people.

Colonel Paschkov joined the group. The Englishman
explained that the Jesus who had helped the woman of
Samaria and Saul was the Son of Man and was still very
much alive. The Englishman quoted a verse from the Bible:
"For the Son of Man is come to save that which is lost"
(Luke 19:10). This amazed Colonel Paschkov, who began to
reflect on how self-centred his whole life had been. Paschkov

was spellbound as he listened to this unlikely Englishman explaining about God's judgement day and the death that Jesus went through on the cross in order to be the Saviour of the world.

When the Englishman had finished speaking Paschkov asked the Prince next to him who the Englishman was. He was told that his name was Lord Radstock and that the Grand Duchess' life had been totally changed after she had met him in Paris.

Later that same evening Colonel Paschkov found himself kneeling down next to Lord Radstock. They had an open Bible between them. Then and there Paschkov committed himself to Jesus Christ, who had been presented to him so lovingly that evening.

PATRICK   *Captive in Ireland*
5th-century missionary bishop in Ireland

I am Patrick, a sinner, most unlearned, the least of all the faithful, and utterly despised by many. My father was Calpurnius, a deacon, son of Potitus, a priest, of the village Bannavem Taburniae; he had a country seat nearby, and there I was taken captive.

I was then about sixteen years of age. I did not know the true God. I was taken into captivity to Ireland with many thousands of people – and deservedly so, because we turned away from God, and did not keep his commandments, and did not obey our priests, who used to remind us of our salvation. And the Lord brought over us the wrath of his anger, and scattered us among many nations, even unto the utmost parts of the earth, where now my littleness is placed among strangers.

And there the Lord opened the sense of my unbelief that I might at last remember my sins and be converted with all my heart to the Lord my God, who had regard for my abjection, and mercy on my youth and ignorance, and watched over me before I knew him, and before I was able to distinguish between good and evil, and guarded me, and comforted me as would a father his son.

The Confession, Patrick, c. 450

PAUL (1) *The Damascus Road*
The apostle Paul, writer of New Testament letters

Meanwhile, Saul was still breathing out murderous threats against the Lord's disciples. He went to the high priest and asked him for letters to the synagogues in Damascus, so that if he found any there who belonged to the Way, whether men or women, he might take them as prisoners to Jerusalem. As he neared Damascus on his journey, suddenly a light from heaven flashed around him. He fell to the ground and heard a voice say to him, "Saul, Saul, why do you persecute me?"

"Who are you, Lord?" Saul asked.

"I am Jesus, whom you are persecuting," he replied. "Now get up and go into the city, and you will be told what you must do."

The men travelling with Saul stood there speechless; they heard the sound but did not see anyone. Saul got up from the ground, but when he opened his eyes he could see nothing. So they led him by the hand into Damascus. For three days he was blind, and did not eat or drink anything.

In Damascus there was a disciple named Ananias. The Lord called to him in a vision, "Ananias!"

"Yes, Lord," he answered.

The Lord told him, "Go to the house of Judas on Straight Street and ask for a man from Tarsus named Saul, for he is praying. In a vision he has seen a man named Ananias come and place his hands on him to restore his sight."

"Lord," Ananias answered, "I have heard many reports about this man and all the harm he has done to your saints in Jerusalem. And he has come here with authority from the chief priests to arrest all who call on your name."

But the Lord said to Ananias, "Go! This man is my chosen

instrument to carry my name before the Gentiles and their kings and before the people of Israel. I will show him how much he must suffer for my name."

Then Ananias went to the house and entered it. Placing his hands on Saul, he said, "Brother Saul, the Lord – Jesus, who appeared to you on the road as you were coming here – has sent me so that you may see again and be filled with the Holy Spirit." Immediately, something like scales fell from Saul's eyes, and he could see again. He got up and was baptised, and after taking some food, he regained his strength.

Acts 9:1–19

PAUL (2)
Paul's second account of his conversion

Persecuted Christians to their death

As the soldiers were about to take Paul into the barracks, he asked the commander, "May I say something to you?"

"Do you speak Greek?" he replied. "Aren't you the Egyptian who started a revolt and led four thousand terrorists out into the desert some time ago?"

Paul answered, "I am a Jew, from Tarsus in Cilicia, a citizen of no ordinary city. Please let me speak to the people."

Having received the commander's permission, Paul stood on the steps and motioned to the crowd. When they were all silent, he said to them in Aramaic:

"Brothers and fathers, listen now to my defence."

When they heard him speak to them in Aramaic, they became very quiet.

Then Paul said: "I am a Jew, born in Tarsus of Cilicia, but brought up in this city. Under Gamaliel I was thoroughly trained in the law of our fathers and was just as zealous for God as any of you are today. I persecuted the followers of this Way to their death, arresting both men and women and throwing them into prison, as also the high priest and all the council can testify. I even obtained letters

173

from them to their brothers in Damascus, and went there to bring these people as prisoners to Jerusalem to be punished.

"About noon as I came near Damascus, suddenly a bright light from heaven flashed around me. I fell to the ground and heard a voice say to me, 'Saul! Saul! Why do you persecute me?'

"'Who are you, Lord?' I asked.

"'I am Jesus of Nazareth, whom you are persecuting,' he replied. My companions saw the light, but they did not understand the voice of him who was speaking to me.

"'What shall I do, Lord?' I asked.

"'Get up,' the Lord said, 'and go into Damascus. There you will be told all that you have been assigned to do.' My companions led me by the hand into Damascus, because the brilliance of the light had blinded me.

"A man named Ananias came to see me. He was a devout observer of the law and highly respected by all the Jews living there. He stood beside me and said, 'Brother Saul, receive your sight!' And at that very moment I was able to see him.

"Then he said: 'The God of our fathers has chosen you to know his will and to see the Righteous One and to hear words from his mouth. You will be his witness to all men of what you have seen and heard. And now what are you waiting for? Get up, be baptised and wash your sins away, calling on his name.'

"When I returned to Jerusalem and was praying at the temple, I fell into a trance and saw the Lord speaking. 'Quick!' he said to me. 'Leave Jerusalem immediately, because they will not accept your testimony about me.'

"'Lord,' I replied, 'these men know that I went from one synagogue to another to imprison and beat those who believe in you. And when the blood of your martyr Stephen was shed, I stood there giving my approval and guarding the clothes of those who were killing him.'

"Then the Lord said to me, 'Go; I will send you far away to the Gentiles.'"

The crowd listened to Paul until he said this. Then they raised their voices and shouted, "Rid the earth of him! He's not fit to live!"

As they were shouting and throwing off their cloaks and flinging dust into the air, the commander ordered Paul to be taken into the barracks.

Acts 21:37–22:24

PAUL (3)   *"I saw a light from heaven"*
Paul relates his conversion experience to King Agrippa

Then Agrippa said to Paul, "You have permission to speak for yourself."

So Paul motioned with his hand and began his defence: "King Agrippa, I consider myself fortunate to stand before you today as I make my defence against all the accusations of the Jews, and especially so because you are well acquainted with all the Jewish customs and controversies. Therefore, I beg you to listen to me patiently.

"The Jews all know the way I have lived ever since I was a child, from the beginning of my life in my own country, and also in Jerusalem. They have known me for a long time and can testify, if they are willing, that according to the strictest sect of our religion, I lived as a Pharisee. And now it is because of my hope in what God has promised our fathers that I am on trial today. This is the promise our twelve tribes are hoping to see fulfilled as they earnestly serve God day and night. O King, it is because of this hope that the Jews are accusing me. Why should any of you consider it incredible that God raises the dead?

"I too was convinced that I ought to do all that was possible to oppose the name of Jesus of Nazareth. And that is just what I did in Jerusalem. On the authority of the chief priests I put many of the saints in prison, and when they were put to death, I cast my vote against them. Many a time I went from one synagogue to another to have them punished, and I tried to force them to blaspheme. In my

175

obsession against them, I even went to foreign cities to persecute them.

"On one of these journeys I was going to Damascus with the authority and commission of the chief priests. About noon, O King, as I was on the road, I saw a light from heaven, brighter than the sun, blazing around me and my companions. We all fell to the ground, and I heard a voice saying to me in Aramaic, 'Saul, Saul, why do you persecute me? It is hard for you to kick against the goads.'

"Then I asked, 'Who are you, Lord?'

"'I am Jesus, whom you are persecuting,' the Lord replied. 'Now get up and stand on your feet. I have appeared to you to appoint you as a servant and as a witness of what you have seen of me and what I will show you. I will rescue you from your own people and from the Gentiles. I am sending you to them to open their eyes and turn them from darkness to light, and from the power of Satan to God, so that they may receive forgiveness of sins and a place among those who are sanctified by faith in me.'

"So then, King Agrippa, I was not disobedient to the vision from heaven. First to those in Damascus, then to those in Jerusalem and in all Judea, and to the Gentiles also, I preached that they should repent and turn to God and prove their repentance by their deeds. That is why the Jews seized me in the temple courts and tried to kill me. But I have had God's help to this very day, and so I stand here and testify to small and great alike. I am saying nothing beyond what the prophets and Moses said would happen – that the Christ would suffer and, as the first to rise from the dead, would proclaim light to his own people and to the Gentiles."

At this point Festus interrupted Paul's defence. "You are out of your mind, Paul!" he shouted. "Your great learning is driving you insane."

"I am not insane, most excellent Festus," Paul replied. "What I am saying is true and reasonable. The king is familiar with these things, and I can speak freely to him. I am convinced that none of this has escaped his notice, because it was not done in a corner. King Agrippa, do you believe the prophets? I know you do."

Then Agrippa said to Paul, "Do you think that in such a short time you can persuade me to be a Christian?"

Paul replied, "Short time or long – I pray God that not only you but all who are listening to me today may become what I am, except for these chains."

Acts 26:1–29

ALEXANDER PAVLOVICH
Tsar of Russia in the time of Napoleon

*Through setting
Moscow alight*

As Tsar, Alexander was in charge of everything, including the church; but his power led to conceit, and he had no religious faith. When he had to appoint a new leader of the church, he chose a school friend, Prince Galitsin, who was young, rich and known for his immoral life.

Galitsin, however, began to suffer pangs of conscience. He read the Gospels, and saw himself afresh as a sinner in God's sight. His conversion brought a complete change to his life: he began to talk about his living Saviour. He asked the Tsar if he had ever read the Gospels. The Tsar had to admit that he had not.

When Alexander watched the rout of his troops by the French in 1806, he was ashamed. He saw the falseness of his life and ambitions, and he thought of Galitsin's conversion. He started to read the Bible for himself, and found a new world opening up.

When Napoleon invaded Russia, the Tsar was no longer arrogant; he was conscious of the cost of the war in the lives of men, and he turned to God in prayer.

Moscow was evacuated, set alight before the French got there, and the Tsar saw it as a metaphor of Christian rebirth: only when he died to himself and gave up everything would he be able to exercise faith in Christ. He prayed the prayer of true repentance.

Napoleon called for the Tsar to seek terms of peace, but

Alexander ignored him and after five weeks the French withdrew, suffering terribly in the Russian winter.

Alexander tackled the army which Napoleon had rebuilt, and when his generals disagreed over tactics Alexander quietly left the room to pray before taking his decision. When Napoleon was defeated, Alexander did not call for reprisals but only for his exile.

At home, the Tsar's remaining years were characterized by his spending much time in prayer; by his support for the Bible Societies of Russia; and by a movement of humility among his people and especially among the different congregations of Christians in the main cities.

PEADA — _Asking for a wife_
7th-century king of the Middle Angles

He was an excellent young man, worthy of being a king, so his father, King Penda, promoted him to rule over the Middle Angles (East Anglia). He came to Oswin, king of the Northumbrians, asking for his daughter Alhflæd in marriage. But the only way he could get her was by becoming a Christian and being baptized together with the nation he ruled.

This was a stumbling-block for Peada only until he learned something about Christianity. He wanted the promise of the heavenly kingdom and the certainty of resurrection and eternal life which the Christian faith promised. He now reached the point where he said that he would have willingly become a Christian even without a bride.

It was King Oswin's son Alhfrith who was mainly responsible for persuading Peada to become a follower of Christ. He was already Peada's friend and also his brother-in-law since he had married his sister Cyneburh, the daughter of king Penda. Peada was baptized by Bishop Finan along with everybody who accompanied him.

Ecclesiastical History of the Nation, Bede, c. 731, Book III, chapter 21

NIKKI PEARCE
Convert from Communism

Personal revolution

Nikki joined the Communist Party of Great Britain without realizing that it was an atheist organization. As she read more and more Communist literature, she came to consider God less and less, and her personality changed so that she was antagonistic to non-Communists.

Then she met a Christian who showed her that Christians could be dedicated workers in the same way that Communists were dedicated to their cause. She read about the less palatable aspects of Communist behaviour, and knew that she too could become someone whose zeal led her to torture and kill. She saw that because Communism was based on a denial of God, it held the possibility of personality changes like this. She became a Christian, allowing Jesus to introduce a personal revolution and make her a new person.

ISAAC PENINGTON
Early Quaker, and neighbour of William Penn

"I have met with my God"

I was acquainted with a spring of life from my childhood, which enlightened me in my tender years, and pointed my heart towards the Lord, begetting the sense in me, and faith, and hope, and love, and humility, and meekness, &c. so that indeed I was a wonder to some that knew me, because of the savour and life of religion which dwelt in my heart, and appeared in my conversation. But I never durst trust the spring of my life ... The Lord was very tender and merciful to me, helping me to pray, and helping me to understand the scriptures, and opening and warming my heart every day ...

When I was broken and dashed to pieces in my religion, I ... could not now hold up an outward form of that which I inwardly wanted: having lost my God, my Christ, my faith, my knowledge, my life, my all ...

The Lord at length had compassion on me, and visited me; though in a time and way wherein I expected him not; nor was I willing (as to the natural part) to have *that* the way, which God showed me to *be* the way; but the Lord opened mine eye, and

179

that which I know to be of him in me closed with it, and owned it ... I sensibly knew and felt my Saviour, and was taught by him to take up the cross, and to deny that understanding, knowledge, and wisdom, which had so long stood in my way: and then I learned that lesson (being really taught it of the Lord), what it is indeed to become a fool for Christ's sake. I cannot say but I had learned somewhat of it formerly; but I never knew how to keep to what I had learned till that day.

Both Isaac and his wife Mary had long been dissatisfied ... each was earnestly seeking after a religion that could bring assurance with it; and each was in no small degree already acquainted with spiritual exercises, and devotions. One day, as they were walking together in a park, a man who had lately attached himself to the people called Quakers, rode by ... and spoke to them of the light and grace of God, which had appeared to all men ... It seems, however, to have been ... by means of the preaching of George Fox, that Isaac Penington became fully satisfied ... "The mystery of iniquity was so opened, and the mystery of the gospel of peace so plainly mainfested, that he (Penington) was fully satisfied; and from that time gave himself up to the obedience of Truth – took up the cross – and suffered with [the Quakers] for the name and testimony of Jesus."...

Whereas we should have pressed forward into the spirit and power, we ran too much outward into the letter and form: and though the Lord in many things helped us, yet therein he was against us, and brought darkness, confusion, and scattering upon us ...
Now what I met with after this, in my travails, in my waitings, in my spiritual exercises, is not to be uttered; only in general I may say this, I met with the very strength of hell ... I have met with my God; I have met with my Saviour ... and my weakness, which I feel in myself, is not my loss, but advantage before him ...

Memoirs of the life of Isaac Penington, Joseph Gurney Bevan, Phillips, 1807, pp. 8–32

PENITENT THIEF
1st-century thief executed alongside Jesus

With Jesus

Two other men, both criminals, were also led out with him to be executed ...

One of the criminals who hung there hurled insults at him: "Aren't you the Christ? Save yourself and us!"

But the other criminal rebuked him. "Don't you fear God," he said, "since you are under the same sentence? We are punished justly, for we are getting what our deeds deserve. But this man has done nothing wrong."

Then he said, "Jesus, remember me when you come into your kingdom."

Jesus answered him, "I tell you the truth, today you will be with me in paradise."

Luke 23:32, 39–43

NIGEL PERRIN
Singer with the King's Singers

Resenting God

His wife having become a Christian, Nigel found himself resenting "this God who was taking my wife away from me". He would not commit himself to Christ because he was afraid of losing control over his life. But he read a hotel Bible while the King's Singers were on tour in South Africa, and he went to the Anglican church near the hotel.

"I sat there among a church full of strangers, yet there was a Person in that building ... I realised who God was and what he meant to me."

Relatives continued to urge him to decide what he was going to do about Jesus. When his sister invited him to come to a service at which she and her fiancé were to be baptized, Nigel said he would be baptized with them.

JOHN PERRY *A "heavy-duty" preacher*
Musician

John Perry met up with many Christians when he went on a Gospel tour with Cliff Richard. He realized that somehow these people were qualitatively different from all the other people he had been used to meeting. Many of the tour's venues were churches, and before it was time for Cliff's spot, which John helped with, he had to listen to the rest of the service and also the sermon.

John remembers one particularly "heavy-duty" preacher. He recalls that what this man said seemed to describe exactly how his life was. The preacher called for people to ask Jesus Christ into their lives. John was most embarrassed about all this, as he was sitting next to his close friends. The preacher asked those who wanted to become Christians to put up their hands, and John's went up involuntarily. The next thing he knew was that he was marching down the aisle with tears streaming down his cheeks. His joy at meeting the Saviour of the world knew no bounds.

MIKE PETERS *Through reading* Countdown
Singer

Mike Peters does not remember much about the details of the book *Countdown* that caused his coming to Christ. He took it with him on a rail journey to Liverpool. The book seemed to be asking one big question: did he want to know about God's gift of eternal life? Mike found that the book explained the meaning of eternal life to him in a very helpful way. He became convinced about the existence of Jesus and had a deep sense of joy as the presence of Christ flooded through him. Anybody observing him would have seen his face streaming with happy tears.

Once when we were going to the place of prayer, we were met by a slave girl who had a spirit by which she predicted the future. She earned a great deal of money for her owners by fortune-telling. This girl followed Paul and the rest of us, shouting, "These men are servants of the Most High God, who are telling you the way to be saved." She kept this up for many days. Finally Paul became so troubled that he turned round and said to the spirit, "In the name of Jesus Christ I command you to come out of her!" At that moment the spirit left her.

When the owners of the slave girl realised that their hope of making money was gone, they seized Paul and Silas and dragged them into the market-place to face the authorities. They brought them before the magistrates and said, "These men are Jews, and are throwing our city into an uproar by advocating customs unlawful for us Romans to accept or practise."

The crowd joined in the attack against Paul and Silas, and the magistrates ordered them to be stripped and beaten. After they had been severely flogged, they were thrown into prison, and the jailer was commanded to guard them carefully. Upon receiving such orders, he put them in the inner cell and fastened their feet in the stocks.

About midnight Paul and Silas were praying and singing hymns to God, and the other prisoners were listening to them. Suddenly there was such a violent earthquake that the foundations of the prison were shaken. At once all the prison doors flew open, and everybody's chains came loose. The jailer woke up, and when he saw the prison doors open, he drew his sword and was about to kill himself because he thought the prisoners had escaped. But Paul shouted, "Don't harm yourself! We are all here!"

The jailer called for lights, rushed in and fell trembling before Paul and Silas. He then brought them out and asked, "Sirs, what must I do to be saved?"

They replied, "Believe in the Lord Jesus, and you will be saved – you and your household." Then they spoke the word of the Lord to him and to all the others in his house. At that hour of the night the jailer took them and washed their wounds; then immediately he and all his family were baptised. The jailer brought them into his house and set a meal before them; he was filled with joy because he had come to believe in God – he and his whole family.

When it was daylight, the magistrates sent their officers to the jailer with the order: "Release those men." The jailer told Paul, "The magistrates have ordered that you and Silas be released. Now you can leave. Go in peace."

But Paul said to the officers: "They beat us publicly without a trial, even though we are Roman citizens, and threw us into prison. And now do they want to get rid of us quietly? No! Let them come themselves and escort us out."

The officers reported this to the magistrates, and when they heard that Paul and Silas were Roman citizens, they were alarmed. They came to appease them and escorted them from the prison, requesting them to leave the city. After Paul and Silas came out of the prison, they went to Lydia's house, where they met with the brothers and encouraged them. Then they left.

Acts 16:16–40

JOSHUA POOLE
19th-century evangelist
Fiddler Joss

"Fiddler Joss" was known as a Wesleyan preacher to the destitute, the alcoholics, the tramps and the street women of the last century. But he had started as a child labourer in the mines of Durham, and he grew up to be a wife-batterer and a habitual drunkard. After years of this kind of behaviour he was sent to prison for six months for attacking his wife, and one of the prison officers spoke to him about his soul at every opportunity.

One day Poole read through the whole of Psalm 51:

184

Have mercy on me, O God,
 according to your unfailing love;
according to your great compassion
 blot out my transgressions.
Wash away all my iniquity
 and cleanse me from my sin.
For I know my transgressions,
 and my sin is always before me.
Against you, you only, have I sinned
 and done what is evil in your sight,
so that you are proved right when you speak
 and justified when you judge.
Surely I have been a sinner from birth,
 sinful from the time that my mother conceived me.
Surely you desire truth in the inner parts,
 you teach me wisdom in the inmost place.
Cleanse me with hyssop, and I shall be clean;
 wash me, and I shall be whiter than snow.
Let me hear joy and gladness;
 let the bones you have crushed rejoice.
Hide your face from your sins
 and blot out all my iniquity.
Create in me a pure heart, O God,
 and renew a steadfast spirit within me.
Do not cast me from your presence
 or take your Holy Spirit from me.
Restore to me the joy of your salvation
 and grant me a willing spirit to sustain me.
Then I will teach transgressors your ways,
 and sinners will turn back to you.
Save me from bloodguilt, O God,
 the God who saves me,
 and my tongue will sing of your righteousness.
O Lord, open my lips,
 and my mouth will declare your praise.
You do not delight in sacrifice, or I would bring it;
 you do not take pleasure in burnt offerings.
The sacrifices of God are a broken spirit;
 a broken and contrite heart,
 O God, you will not despise.
In your good pleasure make Zion propser;
 build up the walls of Jerusalem.
Then there will be righteous sacrifices,
 whole burnt offerings to delight you;
 then bulls will be offered on your altar.

Poole was reduced to fear and trembling after reading this Psalm, but thought it was no use praying. The prison officer spoke to him about Jesus, and Poole felt for the first time the awfulness of his sins. A few days later, still tearful, Poole listened to the prison officer quoting a verse from an old hymn:

> Have you succeeded yet,
> Try, try again.
> Mercy's door is open set,
> Try, try again.

"Before he had finished the verse I found peace and entered my cell that night resting by faith in Christ my Saviour," he recalled. "All night I prayed, I sang and shouted for joy. The man in the next cell heard me singing and praying and although he had not prayed since his childhood, he prayed that night. The next day, I began telling the cooks about Jesus. Some of them laughed, others jeered, but others came to me by themselves and opened their hearts to me."

His wife was cautious about a reunion, having seen his hypocrisy before, but in time they were reunited and toured the country together as he preached to those who shared the sort of life he had known.

CHARLES PREECE *Friendship*
Warden of a home for society's outcasts

It was an evangelistic meeting in Glasgow, and Billy Graham was the speaker. One of the people who met Jesus Christ there was a businessman called Charles Preece. At that meeting he accepted the friendship offered by the risen Lord.

He wanted to share that friendship with others, not by thrusting religion upon them but by being of service to them. So he became a welfare officer, and his Wayfarer House became a refuge for alcoholics, meths drinkers and ex-prisoners.

Author of Christian devotional books

Eugenia, known as Genie, was being taken to task by her childhood friend Ellen Riley in 1949. Even though Ellen was now so different from Genie – she did not drink or smoke and demonstrated great patience – Genie was drawn to Ellen like a magnet. Ellen became the means through which Genie became a Christian. Ellen quoted, in a very severe tone, the words of Jesus from John 14:6: "I am the way and the truth and the life. No-one comes to the Father except through me." Then Genie was treated to a piercing "sermon" from Ellen. Genie was told that when Jesus said these words He was either telling the truth or He wasn't, in which case He must have been a liar and a complete phony. Ellen also told Genie that Jesus said that if we tried to save our lives we would lose them, but that if we lost our lives for Jesus' sake we would find them. Ellen was demanding that Genie should find real life in Jesus Christ for herself.

Genie did not enter the kingdom of God without a struggle. She resisted everything her friend told her. She fell helplessly into a chair crying her eyes out and saying that she wished that she was dead. Then Ellen said, "It would be the most wonderful thing that ever happened to you if the old Genie Price would die right now – this minute, so the new one can be born."

Something snapped deep within Genie's soul. The darkness fell away from her mind and heart and she agreed with Ellen, "Okay, I guess you're right."

Genie's life was then flooded with God's light and she never forgot 2nd October 1949 and the New York City hotel room where this life-bringing conversation had taken place.

PRISONERS IN FINLAND
Hymns in prison

Seven men condemned to death
in the 1918 Finnish Civil War

Seven of the Red Army soldiers were to be shot at dawn on Monday. On the Sunday, when most of them were swearing with frustration, one of their number began to sing a hymn – 'Safe in the arms of Jesus'. He had heard it sung by the Salvation Army a few weeks before, and now he had found – and he told the other soldiers so – that the God his mother had believed in was now his God also. He had found the Saviour and had prayed to Him for forgiveness, as the penitent thief had done on the cross next to Jesus. Hymns and Bible verses had come to his mind to reassure him; and he had been thanking God.

Within a few hours, all seven men had prayed together; they had no Bible, but the Spirit moved each one of them; in tears, they wrote letters home; they finished the night with more singing, and the atmosphere was so changed that even their guards joined in. For at least one of the guards, the morning of execution was the morning he too knew that he could be saved, as he watched the transformation of his charges.

ROGER PULLAN
Hostel fellowship

London solicitor

Roger Pullan's parents were churchgoers and he had been brought up believing that he was a Christian, but it was not until he was studying Criminology at Cambridge that he found himself making a personal commitment. He can identify when it was, although it took place over a period and was not something he was really conscious of until he had completed the change.

He needed somewhere to live while he was studying, and went to investigate a hostel he knew nothing about, called Tyndale House. They asked him if he was confirmed; he told them he was. Then he discovered it was a Christian hostel, indeed an evangelical one where there were prayers before breakfast each morning.

During his first term of living at Tyndale House, God spoke to him through the fellowship of the Christians there. When someone at last asked him if he had committed his life to the Lord, he said 'Yes' without giving it a moment's thought. And only then did he realize that that was exactly what he *had* done – over the preceding weeks, he had come to trust God.

RASHID   *A Gospel of Luke in Arabic*
Arab convert from Islam

In the school holidays Rashid visited an Industrial Fair where there was a multilingual bookstall, run by a European. He bought a Gospel of Luke in Arabic and took it home to read. The story was very unlike the magical accounts he knew in the Qur'ān – this was simple and factual, and sounded truthful. It dealt at length with the death of Christ, which the Qur'ān denied. If Jesus had indeed been raised, thought Rashid, that would make him a greater prophet than Muhammad. He put the book aside, for such thoughts were heresy, but over the next weeks he kept getting it out again to read.

One day at school he heard about a European missionary who held meetings for Arabs in his home; he started going, and spent hours each week studying the Bible with this man. For three years he continued, despite sometimes being locked out of his home because of his father's disapproval. He knew what the cost would be if he became a Christian – he would be permanently disowned by his father, so he would be without a home and his share of the family's wealth; and he would be unable to qualify as a teacher, since his father would see to it that he was expelled from school. But he knew, too, that to give up Jesus Christ would cost him eternal life and his peace of heart, so he gave his life to Christ and was publicly baptized.

IRINA RATUSHINSKAYA
Russian dissident poet

Secretly talking

When she was ten, Irina started talking to God, secretly, at night. To begin with she asked questions. God did not appear to her in a blaze of light; He did not even seem to be answering her questions. But the answers did come – perhaps she found the answer in reading a book the next day, perhaps she felt certain of the answer from within herself.

These things had little obvious effect at the time, though she had a child's unquestioning faith in God's love. Later, as she grew up, she began to wonder whether God could possibly love her. She had never held a Bible, for she was growing up in atheist Soviet Russia. So she knew little about Jesus, and wondered whether she was a Christian after all. But she felt certain that God existed, and that He was kind. She also realized that this meant He wanted her to be kind as well.

When she was given an 18th-century Bible as a present, she had to spend six weeks learning the Old Church Slavonic with its complicated alphabet, before she could read the Bible. And then as she read it she found that all the Christian truths she had guessed at or read about elsewhere were confirmed for her, and everything slotted into place. God was confirming that she was truly a Christian.

CLIFF RICHARD
Pop singer

"It works"

Though brought up in a Bible-reading family, Cliff Richard drifted away from the church and lived for himself, without reference to God except for keeping up some sort of prayer life.

After the death of his father and the interest of a sister and a friend in the Jehovah's Witnesses, Cliff began asking questions. He worried at them in conversations with Christian acquaintances, and slowly he was affected by the warmth of their friendship. His conversion came gradually but definitely – his questioning lessened and he entered into the life of the local church with Jesus Christ as his own Lord and Saviour.

Later he let his faith be known more publicly, telling a packed Billy Graham youth rally at Earl's Court: "Until you have taken the step of asking Christ to come into your heart, life is not really worthwhile. It *works* – it works for me."

BOBBY RICHARDSON
New York Yankee baseball star

Pastor Simpson
explaining salvation

Before Bobby Richardson became a professional baseball player, with such conspicuous success, he was already a Christian.

He was used to going to church with his family, but when he was 14 his mother invited their local minister to visit them so that he could explain the Christain faith to them. Bobby sat with his older and younger sisters while Pastor J. H. Simpson from the Grace Baptist Church in Sumter, South Carolina, told them why Jesus Christ was the Saviour of the world.

Bobby recalls: "We'd all been active in Sunday school and church, but when Pastor Simpson opened the Scriptures with us that Sunday afternoon in 1949, I realised that I knew about Christ but didn't really understand him or have a personal relationship with him."

This was to be Bobby's big day. On that very day he asked Christ to be his own Saviour.

LEGH RICHMOND
19th-century Anglican clergyman,
writer of popular evangelistic tracts

A few months after [his ordination], a most important revolution took place in his views and sentiments, which produced a striking and prominent change in the manner and matter of his preaching, as well as in the general tenor and conduct of his life. This change was not a conversion from immorality to morality; for he was strictly moral, in the usual acceptation of the term. Neither was it a conversion from heterodoxy to orthodoxy; but it was a conversion from orthodoxy in name and profession, to orthodoxy in its spirit ... He began to read [Wilberforce's *Practical View*], and found himself so deeply interested in its contents, that the volume was not laid down before the perusal of it was completed. The night was spent in reading, and reflecting upon the important truths contained in this valuable and impressive work ... He felt a conviction of his own state as a guilty and condemned sinner, and under that conviction, he sought mercy at the cross of the Saviour. There arose in his mind a solemn consciousness that, however outwardly moral and apparently irreproachable his conduct might appear to men; yet *within*, there was wanting that entire surrender of the heart, that ascendancy of God in the soul, and that devotedness of life and conduct, which distinguishes morality from holiness – an assent to divine truth, from its cordial reception into the heart; and the external profession of religion, from its inward and transforming power ... The Bible became the frequent and earnest subject of his examination, prayer, and meditation ... From the study of the Bible, he proceeded to a minute examination of the writings of the Reformers ... and having from these various sources acquired increasing certainty as to the correctness of his recent convictions, and stability in holding them, he found, what the sincere and conscientious inquirer will always find, the Truth; and his heart being interested, he learnt truth through the heart, and believed it, because he felt it.

A Memoir of the Rev. Legh Richmond, T. S. Grimshawe,
Seeley & Burnside, 1828, pp. 25–28

HELEN ROSEVEARE   *Smoky coffee*
Missionary in the Congo

When Helen arrived at Cambridge University during World
War II, she was extremely shy and home-sick, so the invitation she had found in her room was a life-saver: "If you don't
know anyone, and have nowhere to go after supper, come
and have coffee in my room, No. 12, at 8 p.m. – Dorothy."
The evening was a simple sharing of coffee made with some
difficulty over a smoky fire, but it gave Helen a friend.
Dorothy was an outgoing Christian and a member of the
women's Christian Union. That friendship led to Helen's
coming to personal faith in the Lord Jesus Christ and to
assurance of her own forgiveness of sins, and so ultimately to
her going as a missionary to the war-torn Congo.

RICHARD ROTHWEL   *Bowls*
16th-century English clergyman

He was playing at bowls amongst some papists and vain gentlemen, upon a Saturday, somewhere about Rochdale in Lanca-
shire; there comes into the green to him one Mr Midgley, a
grave and godly minister of Rochdale, whose praise is great in
the gospel, though far inferior to Mr Rothwel in parts and
learning; he took him aside and fell into a large commendation of him, at length told him what pity it was, that such a
man as he should be a companion for papists, and that upon
a Saturday, when he should be preparing for the sabbath-day.
Mr Rothwel slighted his words, and checked him for his
meddling.

The good old man left him, went home and prayed privately for him; Mr Rothwel when he was retired from that

company, could not rest, Mr Midgley's words struck so deep in his thoughts. The next day he went to Rochdale church to hear Mr Midgley, where it pleased God to bless that ordinance so, as Mr Rothwel was by that sermon brought home to Christ. He came after sermon to Mr Midgley, thanked him for his reproof, and besought his direction and prayers, for he was in a miserable condition of nature; and under the spirit of bondage he lay for a time, till afterwards, and by Mr Midgley's hands also he received the Spirit of adoption, wherewith he was so sealed, that he never lost his assurance till his dying day. Though he was a man subject to many temptations, the devil assaulting him very much, yet God was mightily with him, that out of his own experience he was able to comfort many. He esteemed and counted Mr Midgley ever afterward for his spiritual father.

The Lives of Two and Twenty English Divines, Samuel Clarke, Underhill & Rothwell, 1660, pp. 86–87

DANIEL ROWLAND
18th-century Welsh preacher

Prayed for in the middle of a sermon

Daniel Rowland's father was Rector of Llangeitho, Cardiganshire. Just before Daniel was due to be ordained he listened to a sermon preached by Griffith Jones in Llandewibrefi. As Daniel stood in the crowd in front of the pulpit he appeared to be totally vain and conceited. When Griffith Jones took note of Daniel he stopped right in the middle of his sermon. In front of everyone he then prayed aloud for Daniel, asking that God would work in his heart and use him to turn many people from darkness to light.

That prayer shook Daniel to his roots. He became a transformed man after it and went on to be a much used preacher and pastor of a 2,000-strong congregation.

Although he became Bishop of Liverpool John Charles Ryle could easily have become Mayor of Macclesfield. He became a celebrated and controversial writer of Christian books.

Ryle gained a double first at Oxford University. Throughout his school and university days he had gone to church and so he knew a great deal in his head about the Christian faith, but he did not know the Lord Jesus Christ in any personal way.

Ryle's memory of the church service that helped him so much was quite vague. It wasn't a particularly different service and Ryle couldn't even remember anything about the sermon. But he did recall that the second Bible reading came from Ephesians chapter 2. Ryle never knew who read this lesson but he clearly remembered that it was read slowly, with particular emphasis being given to verse 8: "It is by grace you have been saved, through faith – and this not from yourselves, it is the gift of God." The reader paused after each phrase of this verse.

More than any sermon, more than any church service, the acceptance of this verse as God's Word to his soul brought Ryle into the kingdom of God and into his own personal relationship with Jesus Christ.

Ryle was ordained on 12th December 1841 at Farnham Castle. He went on to have over 30 books and tracts published over the next 50 years and has been regarded as a champion of evangelicalism ever since. His books *Expository Thoughts on the Gospels* were among Spurgeon's favourite commentaries on the four Gospels.

SAMARITAN WOMAN
She talked with Jesus at a well

Spirit and truth

The Pharisees heard that Jesus was gaining and baptising more disciples than John, although in fact it was not Jesus who baptised, but his disciples. When the Lord learned of this, he left Judea and went back once more to Galilee.

Now he had to go through Samaria. So he came to a town in Samaria called Sychar, near the plot of ground Jacob had given to his son Joseph. Jacob's well was there, and Jesus, tired as he was from the journey, sat down by the well. It was about the sixth hour.

When a Samaritan woman came to draw water, Jesus said to her, "Will you give me a drink?" (His disciples had gone into the town to buy food.)

The Samaritan woman said to him, "You are a Jew and I am a Samaritan woman. How can you ask me for a drink?" (For Jews do not associate with Samaritans.)

Jesus answered her, "If you knew the gift of God and who it is that asks you for a drink, you would have asked him and he would have given you living water."

"Sir," the woman said, "you have nothing to draw with and the well is deep. Where can you get this living water? Are you greater than our father Jacob, who gave us the well and drank from it himself, as did also his sons and his flocks and herds?"

Jesus answered, "Everyone who drinks this water will be thirsty again, but whoever drinks the water I give him will never thirst. Indeed, the water I give him will become in him a spring of water welling up to eternal life."

The woman said to him, "Sir, give me this water so that I won't get thirsty and have to keep coming here to draw water."

He told her, "Go, call your husband and come back."

"I have no husband," she replied.

Jesus said to her, "You are right when you say you have no husband. The fact is, you have had five husbands, and the man you now have is not your husband. What you have just said is quite true."

"Sir," the woman said, "I can see that you are a prophet. Our fathers worshipped on this mountain, but you Jews claim that the place where we must worship is in Jerusalem."

Jesus declared, "Believe me, woman, a time is coming when you will worship the Father neither on this mountain nor in Jerusalem. You Samaritans worship what you do not know; we worship what we do know, for salvation is from the Jews. Yet a time is coming and has now come when the true worshippers will worship the Father in spirit and truth, for they are the kind of worshippers the Father seeks. God is spirit, and his worshippers must worship in spirit and in truth."

The woman said, "I know that Messiah" (called Christ) "is coming. When he comes, he will explain everything to us."

Then Jesus declared, "I who speak to you am he."

Just then his disciples returned and were surprised to find him talking with a woman. But no-one asked "What do you want?" or "Why are you talking with her?"

Then leaving her water jar, the woman went back to the town and said to the people, "Come, see a man who told me everything I ever did. Could this be the Christ?" They came out of the town and made their way towards him ...

Many of the Samaritans from that town believed in him because of the woman's testimony, "He told me everything I ever did." So when the Samaritans came to him, they urged him to stay with them, and he stayed two days. And because of his words many more became believers.

They said to the woman, "We no longer believe just because of what you said; now we have heard for ourselves, and we know that this man really is the Saviour of the world."

John 4:1–30, 39–42

When still a child, the Brahmin Kasturi Sambamurthy was
invested with "the sacred cord" (Yagnopavita), indicating
that he was a Dwija ("twice-born one"). He studied the religions of the world, learned Sanskrit and read the Vedas, the
Hindu sacred writings.

During the Dasara festival of 1912, the Holy Spirit began
to work in his heart. He knew that his prayers as a Brahmin
were all repetitions of Sanskrit prayers. At that time he
started teaching at the Taylor High School, Narsapur, and
also taught the Telugu language to a missionary in Narsapur.
He received a book from Scotland, called *Answers to Prayer*,
but could not understand how the sender knew his name, his
address and how he longed to know what prayer was.

In 1918, he read *Down Water Street*, and found himself
weeping like a child, without knowing why. He wanted
peace. Then came the answer, in the words of Mark 2:10 –
"The Son of Man has power on earth to forgive sins". In his
pride, he objected that he could not believe in the same God
as people who ate pork. If Jesus was omnipotent and Lord
of the universe, he thought, "He will bring me out in spite
of my resistance." Many Christians were praying for him.
He himself prayed, in Telugu, but not in the name of the
Lord Jesus.

One day he was helping a missionary student to translate
the first verses of John's Gospel into Telugu, and suddenly he
saw that Jesus Christ was the Creator of the universe. After
that he began to pray in the name of the Lord Jesus and to
read the Bible to his children, teaching them about God. He
could no longer be content to be a Brahmin.

After three years, the death of his mother and his wife
made it possible for him to come out boldly for the Lord.
Then, after the recovery of one of his daughters who had been
very ill with typhoid fever, he left home, taking her with him,
and was baptized.

DAME CICELY SAUNDERS
Founder of the modern hospice movement

Letting go

Cicely Saunders had her interest in Christianity stimulated when she read a book by John Hadham entitled *Good God*. This caused Cicely's search to start in earnest and she left no stone unturned as she argued with people, thought, started going to church again, and, most of all, as she read avidly.

She acquired a great deal of head knowledge in this way but her heart had not been affected greatly.

During this time Cicely longed for the type of conversion experience that her friends told her of and about which she had read so much.

Then four friends of Cicely's were planning to go on holiday, but on a holiday with a difference, because they planned to have Bible studies and times for praying together each day. They were surprised that Cicely agreed to join them. But Cicely's friends' worst fears were realized: during the Bible studies Cicely mocked them instead of joining in. But one of the ideas they discussed particularly appealed to her: letting go to God. She understood what they were talking about when they said, "Come to God with nothing, because that's all you've got to bring." This made sense at that time because Japan's unconditional surrender to the British was headline news in all the newspapers.

Cicely went to her room after one of these times of prayer and Bible discussion and she prayed, "Oh God, I must have been emotional or not really meaning it when I said I wanted to try and believe and serve you before, but please can it be all right this time?" Cicely recalls that she thought the Lord replied to her, "It's not you who has to do anything. I have done it all." This was Cicely's moment of truth. It was as if God was telling her that everything was all right. She knew that God was now her Saviour.

DICK SAUNDERS
British evangelist

The son of a Baptist lay pastor, Dick Saunders went to church simply in order not to upset his father. But when he was 17 he brought home a girlfriend who came from a home where God was never spoken of. Dick's father, according to his suppertime custom, read a passage of the Bible and prayed. The girlfriend asked about Christianity and said to Dick, "If I'd been in a Christian home as long as you have, knowing how to pray and read the Bible, I'd be a Christian by now – whereas you're miles from God."

From then on they started seriously examining Christianity together, attending a Baptist church, and within a year they were both converted. Dick remembers that the Bible verse that moved him was Romans 5:8 – "God demonstrates his own love for us in this: While we were still sinners Christ died for us." He knew he was a sinner and, sitting in his church pew, he gave his life to God.

FRANCIS SCHAEFFER
Christian apologist

Francis Schaeffer was born in Germantown in Philadelphia, Pennsylvania, in 1912. Schaeffer's parents thought of themselves as Christians, but they were not churchgoers. Francis went to church without his parents. He attended the Presbyterian church, which was known for its liberal teaching. Partly because Schaeffer did not find answers to satisfy him in this church, he became agnostic during his time at high school.

He started to read his Bible out of curiosity. After he had been doing this for six months he discovered that the Bible answered all the questions he had about life. He knew that what the Bible said was true. This was the basis for Schaeffer's complete change, which took place when he was 18 years old.

HENRY F. SCHAEFFER III
Seeking eternal life

Computer chemist, nominated three times for the Nobel Prize for Chemistry

In 1969 Henry received his Ph.D. from Stanford University, but he had not then made what he refers to as "the most important discovery of my life". This discovery was not made in any chemistry laboratory or computer room.

When Henry visited his fiancée Kären Regne Rasmussen in 1965 he was set on a long trail that eventually led him to becoming a Christian. Kären was doing a course that included religion and in one of her lectures a professor asked why Christ drew so many followers around the world, since His life ended in apparent failure and since His first disciples locked themselves away in a room in fear of the authorities – yet within a few weeks they were setting the world on fire with their Christian message and were quite prepared to endure the worst that any persecutors could do to them.

Kären's professor had asked this question not because he was a Christian believer himself but because he wanted to stimulate the minds of those he was lecturing. He even suggested that one possibility was that Christ did really rise from the dead.

Kären related this whole lecture in great detail to Henry, who listened carefully and found it most interesting. Three years later these thoughts came flooding back into Henry's mind after he heard a preacher say on Easter Day that Christianity was a fraud if Christ had not really risen from the dead. After the service Henry went up to the preacher and asked him if he did really believe that Christ rose from the dead. The preacher was more than happy to admit to this.

Henry had been reading books about the resurrection. Some thought it was true while others thought it was false. One fashionable book at the time, called *The Passover Plot*, maintained that Christ never actually died. He fainted on the cross and was taken down in a half-dead state, suffering from loss of blood and dehydration. Then in the cool of the tomb He slowly regained His strength and consciousness. This book did not cut much ice with Henry. He thought that this was so far-fetched in terms of any probabilistic analysis that he wrote it off as being of no use in the argument about whether Jesus did or did not rise from the dead.

Such books as Frank Morison's *Who Moved the Stone?* and F. F. Bruce's *The New Testament Documents: Are They Reliable?* made a much stronger appeal to Henry's mind. He recalls that at this time, "I became convinced that, as a historical fact, it was just overwhelmingly probable that Jesus had risen from the dead."

Henry had still not yet become a Christian but he found himself leading a Bible study. He was hit by this verse in 1 John 5:13: "I write these things to you ... so that you may know that you have eternal life." He did not understand this so he asked the members of the Bible study group what it meant. One of them replied that it was possible to know about eternal life definitely if you put your trust in Jesus Christ.

Henry well remembers what happened after this Bible study: "Within about 24 hours I knew that Jesus had risen from the dead – and that there was a strong historical proof that he was and is Almighty God. I was convinced that he had died to forgive my sins, and that based on what he had done and my belief in him, I was going to heaven."

CHRISTOPHER SEAMAN
Orchestral conductor   *A longer perspective*

Christopher enjoyed the atmosphere of worshipping in Canterbury Cathedral, where he was a chorister as a boy. He was impressed by the devotion of some of the older members of the choir and the clergymen who led the services. These early influences played a most significant part in the steady steps he took towards embracing Christianity for himself.

At Cambridge University he continued to make spiritual

advances and felt that somebody should have told him about Christ before this! Slowly, gradually, Christopher became a dedicated follower of the Lord Jesus Christ.

With his own lengthy conversion experience in mind he once said, "The Bible is full of quick conversions and of gradual ones, of which the disciples are, of course, the outstanding example. We should never fall into the error of creating fashionable formulae for the way God works."

CAROLYN SEXAUER
Converted Mormon
Prayer and study

Carolyn Sexauer was a Mormon for 30 years. For the last two of those years she was teaching a theology class in her church, and in preparing her lessons she both prayed constantly for guidance and studied the Bible carefully.

The guidance she received took the form of being clearer and ever clearer in her own mind that the Bible did not support Mormon doctrine – indeed, that on key issues they were directly contrary to one another. Mormons believed in a multiplicity of gods, the Bible in one God; Mormons believed that the gods had once been men, and that even in heaven the gods had wives. Above all, Mormon doctrine opposed the belief taught in the Bible that people are set right with God simply through faith in what God has done for them.

Finally, Carolyn abandoned Mormonism and found the burden on her heart lifted.

LORD SHAFTESBURY
19th-century social reformer
Sensitive child

It would appear that Shaftesbury's childhood was characterized by neglect from both his parents. The most important person in his young life was a woman who had gone into service at Blenheim Palace. Her name was Mary Millis or possibly Mills. This humble servant from Woodstock went with her mistress Lady Anne, when she married Lord Ashley, and became her housekeeper. Millis not only loved their young child in a way that nobody else ever did in his life, but she also taught him the Christian faith. Each day she taught him a Bible story and would pray with him. It was not long before the young Lord Shaftesbury was able to identify the loving care of Mary with the loving care of the Lord Jesus Christ Himself. This faith in Jesus Christ which this future English Lord had learned from his mother's housekeeper stayed with Lord Shaftesbury throughout his life.

GEORGE BEVERLY SHEA   *Both knees*
Evangelist and Gospel singer

When the Suffields came to George's Dad's home church for evangelistic services George refused to sing or play in front of the people who knew him so well. Even though George was active in singing and playing in Gospel services, he was not really committed to Jesus Christ at that time. The thought of having to go all the way to the front of the church terrified him.

George did, however, attend these meetings and found that he was greatly convinced about sin in his own life for the first time. But he could not summon up the courage to go forward to the front of the church when the time came.

George's Dad was quick to realize that a spiritual battle was raging in his son's heart, and he was very sensitive not to push his son into doing something that he was not able to do.

At the last of these meetings George sat at the back of the church while his Dad was up front, sitting with the evangelist Fred Suffield on the platform. As he had done every night, Fred invited those who wanted to follow Christ to walk to the front of the church.

As the singing started George's Dad came up to George

and, putting his hand on his shoulder, asked him, "Son, do you think tonight might be the night?"

George did and he went forward, walking down with his Dad to the front of the church. There George knelt down on his left knee only. An old Christian lady who knew George saw this and told him, "You needn't think what you've done is any compliment to God. Both knees, Beverly, and get to praying!"

George always remembers this mission with joy, as it marked the start of his life with Christ as his Saviour and Friend.

THOMAS SHEPARD   *Walking in the fields*
17th-century minister in Massachusetts

I heard Mr Dickinson speak in the chapel on the words, "I will not destroy it for ten's sake" (Genesis 19) and was much affected. But I shook this off and fell from God to loose and lewd company, to lust and pride and gaming and bowling and drinking. And yet the Lord left me not, but a godly scholar, walking with me, fell to discourse about the misery of every man out of Christ, that whatever they did was sin.

I did therefore set more constantly upon the work of daily meditation, sometimes every morning but constantly every evening before supper. I took out a little book I have every day into the fields and writ down what God taught me lest I should forget. But it came to my mind that I should do as Christ: when he was in agony he prayed earnestly. And so I fell down in prayer, and being in prayer I saw myself so unholy and God so holy that my spirits began to sink, yet the Lord recovered me and poured out a spirit of prayer upon me for free mercy and pity, and in the conclusion of the prayer I found the Lord helping me to see my unworthiness of any mercy.

Whereupon walking in the fields the Lord dropped this meditation into me: Be not discouraged therefore because thou art so vile, but make this double use of it.

1. Loathe thyself more.

2. Feel a greater need and put a greater price upon Jesus Christ who only can redeem thee from all sin.

Despite all of this I had no assurance Christ was mine.

The Lord therefore brought Dr Preston to preach upon that text, 1 Corinthians 1:30: "Christ is made unto us wisdom, righteousness, sanctification, and redemption." And when he had opened how all the good I had, all the redemption I had, it was from Jesus Christ, I did then begin to prize him and he became very sweet unto me, although I had heard many a time Christ freely offered by his ministry if I would come in and receive him as Lord and Saviour and Husband. I embraced him and gave myself unto him.

I found therefore the Lord revealing free mercy and that all my help was in that to give me Christ and to enable me to believe in Christ and accept of him, and here I did rest.

The Lord made me see that so many as receive him, he gives power to be the sons of God (John 1:12), and I saw the Lord gave me a heart to receive Christ and so the Lord gave me peace.

God's Plot, Thomas Shepard

ERNEST SHIPPAM   *"I'm all right"*
Meat-paste manufacturer

A clergyman once asked Ernest Shippam, "Is your religion really costing you anything? Because, if it isn't, it can't be worth much." It made Shippam pause and reflect, for his church-going was merely part of the routine of life.

When Billy Graham started running an evangelistic campaign at Harringay in 1954, Shippam, who was managing director of the family meat company, went to hear him, to see if it would be suitable for a coachload of his employees to go to. "My attitude was 'I'm all right – but they could do with a bit of religion.'"

To start with, he had reservations about the methods; but

206

he found God making him realize how rotten his life was, and how he needed God's power if he was to put things right. Shippam went forward at that crusade meeting. "I had a feeling it was now or never," he said.

That night brought new life to his relationship with his wife, family and business. His children found their father so different that they actually wanted to see more of him, which was a new experience. He felt able to stand the strain of business because of his faith. He knew for himself the truth of Paul's saying that "if anyone is in Christ, he is a new creation; the old has gone, the new has come!" (2 Corinthians 5:17).

SAMUEL M. SHOEMAKER   *Resentment*
American Episcopal minister and writer

There was a young Chinese businessman in Samuel Shoemaker's class, who was dissatisfied with Buddhism. Shoemaker thought Frank Buchman would be able to help his friend – but Buchman turned the tables and asked why Shoemaker himself did not speak to the youth. What was the obstacle to winning the young man for Christ?

Shoemaker considered. What was the problem? He asked Frank Buchman what he thought it could be.

Buchman confessed that sin had been the reason why he himself had not entered immediately upon the sort of personal evangelism he was now known for. He told Shoemaker that Dr Robert Speer had analysed the fundamentals of the Sermon on the Mount as absolute honesty, absolute purity, absolute unselfishness and absolute love. As he prayed that night, Shoemaker surrendered to God's will. He faced his sins honestly and gave them up to God, as an act of will rather than anything emotional. He felt at at ease about it and soon was able to analyse what he had done.

He had broken with conscious sin, decisively. No longer was he going to go his own way in pride. He set aside time for daily devotions. He put the major decisions of his life in God's hands. And he learned how to witness to other individuals about the experience of conversion and prayer and power.

CHARLES SIMEON
19th-century Cambridge preacher

Passion

It was but the third day after my arrival [as an undergraduate at King's College, Cambridge] that I understood I should be expected in the space of about three weeks to attend the Lord's Supper. "What," said I, "*must* I attend?" On being informed that I must, the thought rushed into my mind that Satan himself was as fit to attend as I; and that if I must attend, I must *prepare* for my attendance there. Without a moment's loss of time, I bought the *Whole Duty of Man*, the only religious book that I had ever heard of, and began to read it with great diligence; at the same time calling my ways to remembrance, and crying to God for mercy; and so earnest was I in these exercises that within the three weeks I made myself quite ill with reading, fasting, and prayer.

The first book which I got to instruct me in reference to the Lord's Supper (for I knew that on Easter Sunday I must receive it again) was Kettlewell on the Sacrament; but I remember that it required more of me than I could bear, and therefore I procured Bishop Wilson on the Lord's Supper, which seemed to be more moderate in its requirements. I continued with unabated earnestness to search out and mourn over the numberless iniquities of my former life; and so greatly was my mind oppressed with the weight of them that I frequently looked upon the dogs with envy; wishing, if it were possible, that I could be blessed with their mortality, and they be cursed with my immortality in my stead. I set myself immediately to undo all my former sins, as far as I could; and did it in some instances which required great self-denial, though I do not think it quite expedient to record them; but the having done it has been a comfort to me even to this very hour, inasmuch as it gives me reason to hope that my repentance was genuine.

My distress of mind continued for about three months, and well might it have continued for years, since my sins were more in number than the hairs of my head; but God in infinite condescension began at last to smile upon me, and to give me a hope of acceptance with Him.

But in Passion Week, as I was reading Bishop Wilson on the Lord's Supper, I met with an expression to this effect – "That the Jews knew what they did, when they transferred their sin to the head of their offering." The thought came into my mind, What, may I transfer all my guilt to another? Has God provided an Offering for me, that I may lay my sins on His head? Then, God willing, I will not bear them on my own soul one moment longer. Accordingly I sought to lay my sins upon the sacred head of Jesus; and on the Wednesday began to have a hope of mercy; on the Thursday that hope increased; on the Friday and Saturday it became more strong; and on the Sunday morning, Easter-day, April 4, I awoke early with those words upon my heart and lips, "Jesus Christ is risen to-day! Hallelujah! Hallelujah!" From that hour peace flowed in rich abundance into my soul; and at the Lord's Table in our Chapel I had the sweetest access to God through my blessed Saviour. I remember on that occasion, there being more bread consecrated than was sufficient for the communicants, the clergyman gave some of us a piece more of it after the service; and on my putting it into my mouth, I covered my face with my hand and prayed. The clergyman seeing it smiled at me; but I thought, if he had felt such a load taken off from his soul as I did, and had been as sensible of his obligations to the Lord Jesus Christ as I was, he would not deem my prayers and praises at all superfluous.

The service in our Chapel has almost at all times been very irreverently performed; but such was the state of my soul for many months from that time that the prayers were as marrow and fatness to me. Of course there was a great difference in my frames at different times; but for the most part they were very devout, and often, throughout a great part of the service, I prayed unto the Lord "with strong crying and tears." This is a proof to me that the deadness and formality experienced in the worship of the Church arise far more from the low state of our graces than from any defect in our Liturgy. If only we had our hearts deeply penitent and contrite, I know from my experience at this hour that no prayers in the world could be better suited to our wants or more delightful to our souls.

Memoirs of the Life of the Rev. Charles Simeon, ed. William Carus, Hatchard, 1848

JAMES SIMPSON *Challenge*
Discoverer of chloroform as an anaesthetic

A patient who was a devout Christian spoke to Dr Simpson about the spiritual poverty of his life, and the challenge proved to be the culmination of years of challenges which he had ignored. This time he repented of his sins, preferring God's forgiveness to the wealth and professional honour he enjoyed. He told his students about his conversion, and described himself as the oldest sinner and youngest believer in the room.

Near the end of his life, he was asked in a public meeting what had been his greatest discovery, and without hesitation he replied, "That I have a Saviour."

SADHU SUNDAR SINGH *In a vision*
Itinerant Indian preacher

Born in 1889, in the Patiala state of North India, Sundar Singh was most influenced in his early life by his Sikh mother. Once a week he was taken to sit at the feet of a sadhu who lived some miles from his home in the middle of a jungle. But Sundar Singh was blessed enough to be sent to a Christian mission school. His mother's idea in this was for him to learn

English, but by the providence of God he also learned about Jesus Christ and His love for everyone in the world.

At the age of 14 Sundar Singh's life was thrown into violent despair by the death of his mother. He took it out on the missionaries who ran the school, making fun of their converts. He then proceeded to burn a Bible, one page at a time, at his home. That night he went to bed planning to take his own life the following day on the railway line.

But before it was light he woke his father and told him that he had had a vision during the night in which he had seen Jesus Christ and had heard His voice. He told his father that he would now spend his life in following Christ to the day he died.

Sundar Singh's father tried to persuade him to renounce his conversion and attempted to poison his own son when he refused to. Sundar Singh spent the remaining 25 years of his life witnessing to to the Lord Jesus Christ, in the teeth of fierce opposition.

BROTHER SIX   *Breaking the powers*
Opium addict in Thailand

Brother Six was a village headman in North Thailand. He was also an opium addict and an animist.

One day, a Christian missionary came to his house, seeking shelter for the night. It was the first time Brother Six had heard of God the Creator, the Father of Jesus Christ who died for man's sake, or the Holy Spirit who could change people's hearts and entrenched attitudes.

When the missionary next called at the same village, he found the headman had become a Christian. He had already begun to break his opium addiction, and now he threw away the symbols of his previous animistic faith – the armbands he wore, the demon-shelf in his house. His wife became a Christian later, and some 13 years after the first missionary visit Brother Six was ordained a Christian minister. His mission was, first, to the surrounding Yao villagers, and then to tribespeople who had forsaken their Communist-ruled homeland. Brother Six started recording messages for them, believing that God had taken them to a country where they could hear the Gospel and become Christian converts.

TOM SKINNER
New York teenage gang leader   *Radio*

Tom Skinner was planning one of the biggest street wars of his life. Then he heard a religious programme on the radio which explained three things to him.

1. Jesus Christ shed His blood to forgive him his sin.
2. Sin stemmed from living a life in independence from God.
3. Christ came alive three days after His death so that He could share His resurrection life with anybody who committed his life to Him.

Tom Skinner could scarcely believe his own actions that night. He found himself in the uncharacteristically humble posture of bowing his head. He was responding to the Jesus Christ he had heard about on the radio. He prayed the following prayer: "Lord, I don't understand all of this, I don't dig You. I don't know what You're at, but I DO know that I need You. And based on that, I now give You the right to take over my life. If these things are true, I give you the right to come inside and live in me."

Tom Skinner was then certain that Christ had come into his life, even though he had no exciting feelings to accompany the most important decision of his life.

MARY SLESSOR
19th-century missionary to Calabar   *Fear of being damned*

Mary Slessor became known as "Mother of all the peoples" on account of her amazing missionary work among the people of Calabar. The way in which she was converted to Christ was one that she vowed never to employ with anybody else and never did so.

Mary grew up with an alcoholic father but a Christian mother. No matter what may have happened during the week Mary and her brothers and sisters were smartly dressed on Sunday mornings and attended church with her mother. Mary was often more interested in fooling about in the church than in paying attention to what was happening in the service.

Mary was befriended by an elderly eccentric widow. One day the widow was talking with Mary in her lounge when she took hold of Mary's hand and held it close to the open fire. She told Mary that her soul would "burn in the lowin' bleezin' fire for ever and ever" if she did not repent. Mary was scared into the kingdom in this way. She was so frightened at the prospect of being eternally damned that she gave her heart to the Lord Jesus Christ.

JAMES SMETHAM   *Atonement*
19th-century Wesleyan minister

James Smetham, a Wesleyan minister, told his son in his last illness, in 1847, "I have had such a sight of my own defects and unfaithfulness, and such a view of the purity and holiness of God, as almost made me despair of finding mercy at the last. I remembered that when your brother John was dying, he was delivered from his last fear by remembering and repeating the verse, 'Jesus, Thy blood and righteousness.' I asked that the hymn-book might be given me; I opened it, and the first lines on which my eyes rested were those commencing, 'Jesus, Thy blood and righteousness.' All my fear, doubt, and distress vanished, when at the reading of that verse I cast my soul on the Atonement; and since that time I have enjoyed perfect peace."

Solzhenitsyn tried to defend Marxism during the early days of his imprisonment, but could not keep it up. Reading Dostoevsky had encouraged him to move closer to his childhood beliefs, seeing the spiritual as more important than the material, and becoming both patriotic and religious. He knew he was not able to solve the complexities of religion, or become a believer, but people who met him thought he believed.

After his experience of cancer and his witnessing the deaths of many other prisoners, he reflected more on the meaning of his own life. Setting out to survive would cost him his spiritual life. It was better to give up seeking material comforts, and to welcome the beneficial effects of prison camp deprivations. He had believed in fate, but he had spelled "god" with a small "g"; now, after his operation, he began to write it with a capital letter: God was working. Suffering helped him to understand what it meant to love his neighbour. A doctor told him how he had been converted from Judaism to Christianity, and it was whilst he was still in the hospital that Solzhenitsyn returned to Christianity. God was still there even though Solzhenitsyn had been denying His existence.

When he was discharged from hospital, he wrote of how faith in God's will and God's mercy had helped him. He wrote a number of prayers, but they were not private, mystical prayers; they expressed faith in God, and confidence that God would help him to do practical things. Later, when he came to live in the United States, his household all wore crosses and observed the church festivals and celebrated Easter and the children's saints' days as more important than Christmas and birthdays. Alexander was not given to mysticism, but had an Orthodox chapel in the house and maintained a firm belief in God.

I sometimes think I might have been in darkness and despair until now had it not been for the goodness of God in sending a snowstorm, one Sunday morning, while I was going to a certain place of worship. When I could go no further, I turned down a side street, and came to a little Primitive Methodist Chapel. In that chapel there may have been a dozen or fifteen people. I had heard of the Primitive Methodists, how they sang so loudly that they made people's heads ache; but that did not matter to me. I wanted to know how I might be saved, and if they could tell me that, I did not care how much they made my head ache. The minister did not come that morning; he was snowed up, I suppose. At last, a very thin-looking man, a shoemaker, or tailor, or something of that sort, went up into the pulpit to preach. Now, it is well that preachers should be instructed, but this man was really stupid. He was obliged to stick to his text, for the simple reason that he had little else to say. The text was, "Look unto me, and be ye saved, all the ends of the earth."

He did not even pronounce the words rightly, but that did not matter. There was, I thought, a glimpse of hope for me in that text. The preacher began thus: "My dear friends, this is a very simple text indeed. It says, 'Look'. Now lookin' don't take a deal of pain. It ain't liftin' your foot or your finger; it is just, 'Look'. Well, a man needn't go to College to learn to look. You may be the biggest fool, and yet you can look. A man needn't be worth a thousand a year to be able to look. Anyone can look; even a child can look. But then the text says, 'Look unto *Me*'. Ay!" said he, in broad Essex, "many on ye are lookin' to yourselves, but it's no use lookin' there. You'll never find any comfort in yourselves. Some on ye say, 'We must wait for the Spirit's workin'.' You have no business with that just now. Look to *Christ*. The text says, 'Look unto *Me*'."

Then the good man followed up his text in this way:

"Look unto Me; I am sweatin' great drops of blood. Look unto Me; I am hangin' on the cross. Look unto Me, I am dead and buried. Look unto Me, I am sitting at the Father's right hand. O poor sinner, look unto Me! Look unto Me!"

When he had gone to about that length, and managed to spin out ten minutes or so, he was at the end of his tether. Then he looked at me under the gallery, and I dare-say, with so few present, he knew me to be a stranger. Just fixing his eyes on me, as if he knew all my heart, he said, "Young man, you look very miserable." Well, I did, but I had not been accustomed to have remarks made from the pulpit on my personal appearance before. However, it was a good blow, and it struck right home. He continued, "and you always will be miserable – miserable in life and miserable in death – if you don't obey my text; but if you obey now, this moment you will be saved." Then lifting up his hands, he shouted, as only a Primitive Methodist could do, "Young man, look to Jesus Christ. Look! Look! Look! You have nothing to do but to look and live."

I saw at once the way of salvation. I knew not what else he said – I did not take much notice of it – I was so possessed with that one thought. Like as when the brazen serpent was lifted up, the people only looked and were healed, so it was with me. I had been waiting to do fifty things, but when I heard that word, "Look!" what a charming word it seemed to me! Oh! I looked until I could almost have looked my eyes away. There and then the cloud was gone, the darkness had rolled away, and that moment I saw the sun; and I could have risen that instant, and sung with the most enthusiastic of them, of the precious blood of Christ, and the simple faith which looks alone to Him.

Oh, that somebody had told me this before, "Trust Christ, and you shall be saved." Yet it was, no doubt, all wisely ordered, and now I can say –

Ere since by faith I saw the stream
Thy flowing wounds supply,

216

Redeeming love has been my theme,
And shall be till I die.

C. H. *Spurgeon's Autobiography*, Passmore & Alabaster, 1897, vol. i, pp. 98–100

SPURGEON CONVERT (1) *Crossing over*
A horse-and-van driver *London Bridge*

A man came to join the church; and, according to our usual custom, he was asked how he had become converted, when he told us the following story. He said:

> I was employed in driving a horse and van; I never thought of going to any place of worship, and I do not think anybody ever said a word to me about God or Christ until one day when I was crossing over London Bridge when, suddenly, a man jumped up, and climbed into the back of my cart. I took my whip to lash him off, but he said, "Hold hard, mate, I've got a message for you."
>
> This was a very curious thing to me, and I asked, "What is it?"
>
> "I will tell you, but I may as well sit in front."
>
> So he sat down beside me. Then I asked him, "What is your message?"
>
> "It is a message from God to your soul."
>
> I cursed and swore at him; but that made no difference to him. He said, "You are the very man I was after. I knew you were a swearing man, for it was that first attracted my attention to you, and I am sure my message is for you."
>
> I said to him then, "What have you to say? Come, cut it short."
>
> He did cut it short, and he put it pretty straight, too. He told me what would become of my soul if I died a swearer, and he talked to me about the world to come. Then he told me that there was a Saviour for sinners, and that, if I trusted Him, I should be saved. Before he left me, he made me promise that I would go to hear you, sir. So I promised, and as I always boasted that I kept my word, I came to hear you, though I was precious sorry that I had promised to do so.
>
> I never got up so early on a Sunday morning before; and when the man saw me at the gate, he took me in, and gave me his seat, and stood himself all the service, which I thought was

very kind on his part. After the sermon, he asked me, "Did you like it?"

I replied, "No, I did not; that is not the sort of thing that I care about; I don't believe in religion."

"Ah! but you will," the man said; and he and I parted company at the gate, and I hoped I should never meet him again.

I did not see him for some weeks; but, one day, as I was walking down the Blackfriars Road, I saw him coming along, so I slipped round the first corner, and began to run to avoid him; but, soon, I heard somebody running after me, and he came up to me, and said, "Well, mate, how are you?"

"All right."

"Are you going on any better?" he asked.

I did not give him any answer, and then he told me that he had made up his mind that I should be a Christian one day, and that he never meant to let me alone till that came to pass. I believe he would have gone into my house with me; but, as my wife and I were fond of drink, there was only a little furniture in it, and I did not wish him to come in, and see the miserable place, so, to get rid of him, I proposed to go and hear Mr Spurgeon on the next Sunday. I kept my promise; and, now, I am happy to say that I do not need anybody to induce me to go to the Tabernacle. I have been here six months, I have found the Saviour for myself, and I have got four of our men to come down to hear the gospel with me."

C. H. Spurgeon's Autobiography, Passmore and Alabaster, 1900, vol. iv, p. 41

SPURGEON CONVERT (2)
A man of excellent character

In darkness for 20 years

Perhaps, next to the joy of actual conversions, the rescue of those who have been long in dense spiritual darkness has given me the greatest delight ...

I remember ... a man of excellent character, well beloved by his family, and esteemed by his neighbours, who was for twenty years enveloped in unutterable gloom. He ceased to attend the house of God, because he said it was of no use; and although always ready to help in every good work, yet he had an abiding conviction upon him that, personally, he had no part nor lot in the matter, and never could have. The more anyone talked to him about the things of God, the worse he became; even prayer seemed but to excite him to more fearful despondency.

In the providence of God, I was called to preach the Word in his neighbourhood; he was induced to attend, and, by the Holy Spirit's blessing on the sermon, he obtained a joyful liberty. After twenty years of anguish and unrest, he ended his weary roamings at the foot of the cross, to the amazement of his neighbours, the joy of his household, and the glory of God. Nor did his peace of mind subside; for, until the Lord gave him a happy admission into eternal rest, he remained a vigorous believer, trusting and not being afraid.

C. H. *Spurgeon's Autobiography*, Passmore and Alabaster, 1900, vol. iv, p. 42

SPURGEON CONVERT (3)   *A hopeful patient*
A man who was almost insane

Some years ago, I was the subject of fearful depression of spirit. Various troublous events had happened to me; I was also unwell, and my heart sank within me. Out of the depths I was forced to cry unto the Lord. Just before I went away to Mentone for rest, I suffered greatly in body, but far more in soul, for my spirit was overwhelmed. Under this pressure, I preached a sermon from the words, "My God, My God, why hast Thou forsaken Me?"

I was as much qualified to preach from that text as ever I expect to be; indeed, I hope that few of my brethren could have entered so deeply into those heart-breaking words. I felt to the full of my measure the horror of a soul forsaken of God. Now, that was not a desirable experience. I tremble at the bare idea of passing again through that eclipse of soul; I pray that I may never suffer in that fashion again unless the same result should hang upon it.

That night, after the service, there came into my vestry a man who was as nearly insane as he could be to be out of an asylum. His eyes seemed ready to start from his head, and he said that he should utterly have despaired if he had not heard that discourse, which had made him feel that there was one man alive who understood his feelings, and could describe his experience. I talked with him, and tried to encourage him, and asked him to come again on the Monday night, when I should have a little more time to speak with him. I saw the brother again, and I told him that I thought he was a hopeful patient, and I was glad that the word had been so suited to his case. Apparently, he put aside the comfort which I presented for his acceptance, and yet I had the consciousness upon me that the precious truth which he had heard was at work upon his mind, and that the storm of his soul would soon subside into a deep calm.

Now hear the sequel.

Last night, of all the times in the year, when, strange to say, I was preaching from the words, "The Almighty hath vexed my soul," after the service, in walked this self-same brother who had called on me five years before. This time, he looked as different as noonday from midnight, or as life from death. I said to him, "I am glad to see you, for I have often thought about you, and wondered whether you were brought into perfect peace." I told you that I went to Mentone, and my patient also went into the country, so that we had not met for five years.

To my enquiries, this brother replied, "Yes, you said I was a hopeful patient, and I am sure you will be glad to know that I have walked in the sunlight from that day till now. Everything is changed and altered with me."

Dear friends, as soon as I saw my poor despairing patient the first time, I blessed God that my fearful experience had prepared me to sympathise with him and guide him; but last night, when I saw him perfectly restored, my heart overflowed with gratitude to God for my former sorrowful feelings. I would go into the deeps a hundred times to cheer a downcast spirit: it is good for me to have been afflicted that I might know how to speak a word in season to one that is weary.

C. H. Spurgeon's Autobiography, Passmore and Alabaster, 1900, vol. iv, p. 42

SPURGEON CONVERT (4)
A man intending to commit suicide

Two of our brethren, both working-men – one of whom has
been a famous runner, and who has won prizes in many
running-matches – are accustomed, as they say, to hunt in
couples for souls. Their usual method is for one to go on
one side of the street, and his friend on the other, on the
Lord's-day morning, in those parts of London where Sabbath trading is carried on to the greatest extent. One morning, one of them was giving a tract to a person as the other
was crossing over to join him, to communicate with him
on some subject. As the second friend met the man who
had received the tract, he heard him say, with an oath,
"What is the use of giving me this tract? I shall be in hell
in an hour!"

He said this to his fellow-labourer, on reaching him, "Did
you hear what that man said?"

"No," he answered, "I did not notice; what was it?"

"He appeared very wild, and talked of being in hell in an
hour; he is either insane, or he is intending to commit
suicide."

"Do you think so? Then we will be after him."

They followed him, and the second one, on coming up to
the man, said to him, "What did you say when you took that
tract?"

"That's no concern of yours," he answered, "mind your
own business."

"Oh!" was the reply, "but it is my business, for, if I
heard aright, you said that you would be in hell in an
hour."

"Yes, I did say so; this world is worse than hell, and I'll be
out of it in an hour."

"No, you won't," said our friend, "for I mean to stick by
you; and I won't leave you for an hour, go where you
may."

The poor creature then succumbed, and the godly men
took him into a coffee-shop, and gave him a good break-

fast. The man felt less like committing suicide after that meal. Our friends knew that the best gospel sermon would not be likely to benefit a man who was starving; he had tasted nothing for three days, and had walked the streets all night. Hence, our brethren wisely felt that they must first feed his hungry body; and after that, they brought him to the Tabernacle.

When the service was over, their poor patient looked a little more hopeful, and the soul-doctors thought it best to repeat the dose of solid nutriment. They took him to a house where they were accustomed to dine, in a humble way, and he shared their meal. He went to one of the Bible-classes in the afternoon; and, in the evening, they brought him again to the Tabernacle, and it pleased God to touch the poor man's heart, and bring him to a knowledge of himself and his Saviour. Then he became communicative, and it appeared that he had left his wife for four or five months, and had been living a life of dissipation, sin, and poverty.

He gave the name and address of his wife, in the North of England; she was written to, and his fare was paid home; and, after he had gone back, a letter came from the good woman, saying that she had been a member with the Wesleyan Methodists, and had been long praying for her husband, who had been an awful reprobate, and had at last run away from home. Then she thought it was all over with him; but God had designs of love towards him, and now he had sat down at the Lord's table with her. She did not know what to say, her heart was so full of gratitude to God, and to the dear friends who had been the means of bringing her husband to the Saviour.

C. H. *Spurgeon's Autobiography,* Passmore and Alabaster, 1900, vol. iv, p. 40

SPURGEON CONVERT (5) *A new song*
A ten-year-old boy

The following pleasing testimony came to Mrs Spurgeon on the first anniversary of his home-going:

> More than thirty-nine years ago, when he was a youth of nineteen, and I was a child of ten, I heard him preach a never-to-be-forgotten sermon, which was like an echo upon earth of the "new song" of heaven.
>
> I was in great distress of soul at the time, and had just given myself up as a hopeless backslider, when he came to our little chapel, and preached this lovely sermon. The text was, "And they sang a new song." Vividly, as though it only happened yesterday, do I recall every part of that service, and the heavenly smile lighting up his dear young face, as, looking round into our pew, he seemed to single me out, and said, "Have *you* learned the key-note of that song? I'll tell you in a whisper what it is, 'tis Jesus! only Jesus." And then he went on ringing "those charming bells" of "free grace and dying love" till my poor heart was lifted up into joy, and peace, and full assurance, which, through all the ups and downs of thirty-nine years of spiritual life, I have never quite lost ...
>
> I have often wished to tell your dear one all this; but now, in your dark days, I feel I must tell you. May "the consolations of God" indeed abound towards you!

C. H. *Spurgeon's Autobiography*, Passmore and Alabaster, 1900, vol. iv, p. 44

SPURGEON CONVERT (6) *A prodigal son*
A thief

A conversion related by a Congregational minister in Australia:

> Some years ago, a father, living in a country town, apprenticed his son to a London Silversmith. For a time, all seemed to be going well; but, one day, he received a letter to say that the lad had robbed his master. With a sad heart, he hastened to town only to find, alas! that it was but too true. The indentures were cancelled, and the boy left his situation in disgrace. As the father and son were walking through the crowded streets of the City,

the lad suddenly darted away, and disappeared. The police searched for him in vain, and the poor man had to return alone to tell the sad news to his broken-hearted wife.

Years passed, and nothing was heard of the prodigal son. One Sabbath evening, the parents stayed home from the service; and, while sitting quietly reading God's Word, they were unusually constrained to pray for their lost boy; and they knelt down together, and asked that he might be arrested in his sinful career, and brought back to the old home. Presently, the servant came back from the service she had attended, and her master enquired as to the sermon she had heard. "Oh, sir!" she said, "I have not heard a word of the sermon; I could do nothing but pray for Master Harry."

That night, some men were passing the Metropolitan Tabernacle, on their way to break into the shop of a certain blacksmith in London, when one said to another, "Harry, just run up the steps, and see the time." He did so, opened the door, and stood in the aisle. Mr Spurgeon was preaching about the dying thief; and, seeming to point direct at Harry, said, in those ringing, well-remembered tones, "If there is a thief here tonight, Jesus Christ can save him."

The arrow hit the mark. Harry went back to his garret to pray; and, in a week's time, there was a knock at the front door of his old home in that country town. The father opened it, stood face to face with his long lost son; and then followed the old story of the prodigal's return – tears, confession, forgiveness, welcome, restoration, joy.

C. H. *Spurgeon's Autobiography*, Passmore and Alabaster, 1900, vol. iv, p. 47

JOHN STAM
Missionary to China   *Helpless to help himself*

One definition of conversion is as follows. Conversion is the process, gradual or sudden, by which a self, hitherto divided, consciously wrong and unhappy, becomes unified, consciously right and happy, through its acceptance of divine realities.

This is an accurate description of what happened to John Stam. As a boy of fifteen John had been burdened by the weight of his own sin. His soul became even more alive to God when he heard a blind evangelist preaching at a special evangelistic service. He now knew that he was helpless to help himself and that the only solution to his problem of sin was Jesus Christ. The reality of hell stretched out before him and John felt the horror of standing in all his impurity and sin before the holy God who would one day judge him. John points back to this time as his conversion experience as he then put his trust in the forgiveness of Christ for his sins and subsequently became a godly and God-fearing Christian.

NORMAN STONE
Film director

Visible difference

Norman's father and many of his uncles were Baptist ministers. This made Norman put his guard up against being converted.

But by the time he was 17 he decided to think more carefully about Jesus Christ. He now found that going to church had more meaning to it than mere duty. He discovered that the sermons had messages in them for his heart.

Norman did then ask Christ into his life but it took him three months before he told his parents.

When Norman did tell his mother she was not in the least surprised and said, "Yes, I know; it happened three months ago, didn't it?" Norman's changed life spoke volumes about his newly discovered Friend and Saviour.

JOHN STOTT
Minister and theologian

About 10 p.m. on 13th February 1938

At Rugby School John Stott sometimes went by himself into the school's Memorial Chapel where he tried to pray and read Christian books. At times he went along to a Christian club in his school. At one of these meetings, the speaker was the Rev Eric Nash (or "Bash" as everyone called him). John Stott was so interested that after the meeting he went to talk to "Bash". Recognizing someone who was seeking God, "Bash" took the schoolboy for a car ride, answering his questions, and showing him the way to Christ.

That night, in his school dormitory, John Stott asked Christ into his life. He still has the diary in which he recorded this momentous event. He wrote that up to then, Christ had been on the circumference of his life and he had merely asked Christ to guide him. But now he was giving Christ complete control. He had heard Christ standing at the door and knocking, and he had invited Him into his life, to cleanse it and rule over it.

The next day John wrote in his diary that he had had immense and new joy during the day. He now knew that God ruled him, and that he had never really known God before.

For the next five years, Stott received a weekly letter from "Bash" through which the young believer was encouraged in his life with the Lord Jesus Christ.

C. T. STUDD   *Yielded*
Cricketer and missionary

His housemaster at Eton said of him, "He is incomparably the best cricketer in the Eton and Harrow team of 1879," of which he was captain.

Going up to Trinity in 1879, Studd won his blue and thus played for Cambridge for four consecutive years. He played for Middlesex and for the MCC against the Australians, and in 1882, had the highest batting average of the year, and in bowling, though only fifteenth in the averages, had the second highest number of wickets taken.

When Studd's conversion came it came suddenly. His father had been converted under the ministry of Moody. While the three Studd brothers were at Eton, their father daily prayed that they would become Christians. He did not cease to persuade them about Christ until each of them had turned to Him. None of the three brothers knew what the other two had done until they received a joint letter from their father.

Remembering his conversion experience C. T. Studd said, "I had joy and peace in my soul. I knew then what it is to be 'born again', and the Bible, which had been so dry to me before, became everything."

Convinced that "I had kept myself back from Him, and had not wholly yielded," Studd went down on his knees and from the bottom of his heart said the words of Frances Ridley Havergal's hymn:

> Take my life and let it be
> Consecrated Lord to Thee.

JOHN A. SUBHAN
Convert from Islam

Reading the Gospel story

When John Subhan was seeking for the truth about God with all his heart he was given a copy of the Gospel story. The first time he read it its ethical teaching left its mark on John's thinking. The second time he read it he realized that he was reading God's inspired revelation about His Son, Jesus Christ. John wrote: "The Gospel spoke to me in my mother tongue, whispering to me the secrets of God ... The Gospel dovetailed into my soul, and in the person of Christ that it presented, I found the object of my deeper and inner urge, and the unsatisfied longing of my heart."

DAVID SUCHET
British actor

Gideon Bible

David Suchet's father was Jewish, his mother a nominal Christian. They sent their son to boarding school when he was seven, and both at prep. school and at Wellington he was put off Christianity. The Bible was merely something to be got up for examinations.

Astrology appealed to him, and for a while he would take

no decision without first consulting the tarot. He went to a spiritualist church and met mediums. But as he thought about life after death and whether the deceased grandfather he felt so close to was still living on in some other life, he thought he would like to read the Bible. The very idea of doing so fascinated him. The Bible was being advertised when he switched on his hotel television in America, and he looked for the usual Gideons' Bible, but the bedside drawer was empty. He went out and, feeling very embarrassed about it, bought a New Testament. He came back to his hotel room, went to put the book away in the bedside drawer – and found a Gideons' Bible there where he had looked previously. The oddity of it struck him.

He seemed to be guided in his reading of the New Testament, starting with Acts. When he came to Romans, he read it not as a mere intellectual exercise but as a way of being.

Now the Bible was not just for exams. It contained everything he had been looking for. Other ways were nonsensical; this made sense. He started on the Gospels, wanting to know about Jesus. If only he could live like this! He knew he was not like that, and he grew depressed for many months, but then he came to realize that God did not work the way a chemical equation works, and his concern over his failure was taking him further from God.

He was now struggling both emotionally and intellectually with doubts – but John's Gospel finally cemented his faith by showing him that Jesus could liberate him from his negative self-absorption.

JOHN SUNG
"China's greatest evangelist"

Through the "Hinghwa
Pentecost"

John Sung was born in 1901 in a district of south-east China known as Hinghwa. At the tender age of nine John attended a meeting of the Hinghwa revival, which became known as the "Hinghwa Pentecost" because of the great blessing that

so many people received from it. The young Sung was so convicted of his own sin that he hung his head and cried until his
tears went through his coat to his body. He became a follower of Christ. Later in his life God enabled John Sung to
spark off many such revivals through his own work and
prayers.

HARRY SUTTON   *Always religious*
Former General Secretary of the
South American Missionary Society

"I've always been religious. I love just sitting in a cathedral."
The man who said that, and whose parents brought him up to
sing in the church choir and go to Sunday School regularly,
was 18 before he made a conscious decision to become a
Christian.

Scottish evangelist Andrew Douglas was speaking at an
evangelistic campaign in Liverpool, and this was the first
time Hary Sutton had heard the Gospel message clearly
proclaimed. On Saturday night he responded to the
evangelist's appeal – and on Monday he took his parents
to hear the evangelist too. They were, he says, "gloriously
converted".

After his conversion he would spend his lunch-times in a
coil of rope on the dockside near his office. "That coil of rope
became as precious to me as any cathedral anywhere in the
world. There the Lord and I got on very good terms with each
other."

NIGEL SYLVESTER   *Learning the basics*
Former General Director of the
Scripture Union

Nigel Sylvester identifies two key factors in his conversion
while at Cambridge University. The first was the nightly
preaching in the University church of Great St Mary's,

where the famous preacher Donald Grey Barnhouse and his conviction and power were something new for Sylvester. The second was a mission service after which there was a chance to talk late into the night, learning how to receive Christ personally and then making an individual response in the privacy of one's bedroom.

Christian friends and formal Bible study meetings then taught young converts the foundations of theological understanding – and students were being converted almost every week.

P. V. TABBUSH
Jewish convert

Messiah recognized

Tabbush's father was a Sephardic Jew in Manchester, where his son was born in 1883. The boy learned Hebrew and went to a Jewish boarding school. In 1896 he went to Clifton College, the only school that had an orthodox Jewish house where the Jewish religion could be kept and where there was neither work nor any games on the Sabbath. At Clifton he had his Barmitzvah, the coming-of-age of a male Jew, when he takes responsibility to God for his sins. Tabbush was considered quite religious by his friends, although he admits he did not keep the Sabbath or the whole law.

Many years later, he was introduced to the New Testament by reading *Grace and Truth* by Dr Mackay; the first chapter of the book was called "There is no difference", and showed Tabbush that, no matter how religious he was, or what other people thought of him, he was a guilty sinner in God's sight.

He went to meetings and met Christian believers, but it was not until some time later that he saw that Jesus of Nazareth was the Jewish Messiah, the Son of God and the Saviour of the world, the fulfilment of all the Old Testament prophecies. In September 1942 he accepted Jesus Christ personally, confessing to God that he deserved punishment for his sins, but asking for forgiveness through the merits of Christ crucified.

JAMES HUDSON TAYLOR
Missionary in China

A mother's prayer

He seemed a bright, happy lad of seventeen, but in fact he was rebellious and unbelieving. At the bank in Barnsley where he worked, most of his colleagues were entirely unreligious. One of the older men took every opportunity to laugh at Hudson's "old-fashioned notions", trying to get him to become as frivolous as he was. The lad began to want entertainment, money and a horse to go hunting with his friends. He found it tiresome trying to continue to behave as a Christian, though he did try to for a while.

After a time, he got inflammation of the eyes through doing overtime with gaslight, and he had to leave the bank and return to his father's shop.

He was still unhappy, and his parents could see that all was not well. His father tried to help, but grew impatient with him. His mother understood him better, and worked and prayed for him. But it was his thirteen-year-old sister Amelia he could speak to most freely. She resolved to pray three times a day for his conversion. She did so for some weeks, praying by herself and noting in her diary that she would carry on praying for him until he was brought into the light, and that she believed her petitions would be answered before long.

So, held by the faith and prayers of those who loved him, he came to the day of which he wrote years later:

My mother being absent from home, I had a holiday, and in the afternoon looked through my father's library to find some book with which to while away the unoccupied hours. Nothing attracting me, I turned over a basket of pamphlets and selected from amongst them a Gospel tract that looked interesting, saying to myself, "There will be a story at the commencement and a sermon or moral at the close. I will take the former and leave the latter for those who like it."

231

I sat down to read the book in an utterly unconcerned state of mind, believing indeed at the time that if there were any salvation it was not for me, and with a distinct intention to put away the tract as soon as it should seem prosy.

Little did I know at the time what was going on in the heart of my mother, seventy or eighty miles away. She rose from the dinner table that afternoon with an intense yearning for the conversion of her boy; and feeling that, absent from home and having more leisure than she could otherwise secure, a special opportunity was afforded her of pleading with God on my behalf. She went to her room and turned the key in the door, resolved not to leave the spot until her prayers were answered. Hour after hour that dear mother pleaded, until at length she could pray no longer, but was constrained to praise God for that which His Spirit taught her had already been accomplished, the conversion of her only son.

I in the meantime had been led in the way I have mentioned to take up this little tract, and while reading it was struck with the phrase: "The finished work of Christ".

"Why does the author use this expression?" I questioned. "Why not say the atoning or propitiatory work of Christ?"

Immediately the words "It is finished" suggested themselves to my mind.

What was finished?

And I at once replied, "A full and perfect atonement and satisfaction for sin. The debt was paid for our sins, and not for ours only, but also for the sins of the whole world."

Then came the further thought, "If the whole work was finished and the whole debt paid, what is there left for me to do?"

And with this dawned the joyful conviction, as light was flashed into my soul by the Holy Spirit, that there was nothing in the world to be done but to fall down on one's knees and, accepting this Saviour and His salvation, praise Him for evermore.

Thus while my mother was praising God on her knees in her chamber, I was praising Him in the old warehouse to which I had gone alone to read at my leisure this little book.

Several days elapsed before I ventured to make even my sister the confidante of my joy, and then only after she had promised not to tell anyone. When Mother returned a fortnight later I was the first to meet her at the door and to tell her I had such a glad news to give. I can almost feel that dear mother's arms round my neck as she said,

"I know, my boy."

"Why," I asked in surprise, "has Amelia broken her promise? She said she would tell no one."

My mother assured me that it was not from any human source she had learned the tidings, and went on to tell the incident mentioned above. You will agree with me that it would be strange indeed if I were not a believer in the power of prayer.

Nor was this all. Some time after, I picked up a pocket-book exactly like my own and, thinking it was mine, opened it. The lines that caught my eye were an entry in the little diary belonging to my sister, to the effect that she would give herself daily to prayer until God should answer in the conversion of her brother. One month later the Lord was pleased to turn me from darkness to light.

Brought up in such a circle and saved in such circumstances, it was perhaps natural that from the commencement of my Christian life I was led to feel that the promises were very real, and that prayer was in sober matter of fact transacting business with God, whether on one's own behalf or on the behalf of those for whom one sought His blessing.

This changed Hudson Taylor's whole life; from now on he enjoyed consciously God's acceptance of him, not on the ground of anything he could do or be, but simply because of what the Lord Jesus was and had done. "Not I, but Christ" freed him and gave him joy and peace. A new life began that would in time take him to China.

The Growth of a Soul, Dr and Mrs Howard Taylor, OMF, 1915, pp. 58–61

GEORGE THOMSON   *A month to live?*
18th-century clergyman, friend of Methodism

Shortly after becoming rector of St Gennys, Cornwall, in 1732, George Thomson had a dream. Three times it came to him in one night, suggesting that he had only a month to live. In urgent response, the waking rector asked his friends and parishioners to give him leave of absence from his duties while he sought God. He shut himself up with his Bible, but found only condemnation in its pages. After a fortnight, he came to Romans 3, and came to hope and trust in Jesus "whom God hath set forth to be a propitiation through faith in his blood, to declare his righteousness for the remission of sins that are past". Thomson remained alone with God until he felt sure of his salvation.

Later he was to meet Wesley and Whitefield – the latter recalling how in St Gennys "many, many prayers were put up, by the worthy rector and others, for an outpouring of God's blessed Spirit. They were answered. Arrows of conviction flew so thick and so fast, and such a universal weeping prevailed from one end of the congregation to the other, that good Mr Thomson could not help going from seat to seat, to encourage and comfort the wounded souls."

ARTHUR THURSTON   *Not satisfied*
Converted Jehovah's Witness

Arthur Thurston passed through periods of allegiance to both Anglican and Roman Catholic churches, but was not satisfied. After visits by Jehovah's Witnesses, he became convinced by their arguments, which appeared to be based on the Bible, and he spent many hours each week engaging in doorstep evangelism.

But some neighbours started evengelizing *him*. The couple, who had been recently converted after a long spiritual search, had many discussions with Thurston over a period of two months before inviting him to the mission hall where they worshipped. At a Bible study meeting there, the speaker showed how Jesus wanted people to be sanctified, and offered eternal life to those who believed and would yield themselves to Him.

That night, Arthur Thurston trusted Jesus; his wife followed suit a few days later; and neither of them lived in fear thereafter, for they knew God's love in their hearts.

LEO TOLSTOY
Russian novelist

Changed direction

Tolstoy wrote: "Five years ago I came to believe Christ's teaching, and my life suddenly changed: I ceased to desire what I had previously desired, and began to desire what I formerly did not want. What had previously seemed good to me seemed evil, and what had seemed evil seemed good. It happened to me as it happens to a man who goes out on some business and on the way suddenly decides that the business is unnecessary, and returns home. All that was on his right is now on his left, and all that was on his left is now on his right; his former wish to get as far as possible from home has changed into a wish to be as near as possible to it. The direction of my life and my desires became different, and good and evil changed places."

LORD TONYPANDY
**George Thomas, former Speaker
of the House of Commons**

A public declaration

Every week George went with his family to the Methodist Chapel in Tonypandy in Wales. Once a year, there was a special Youth Sunday which George always enjoyed. When he was 16, the service was held in the meeting room at nearby Trealaw and the speaker was the Rev W. G. Hughes. George never forgot that evening. Complete silence fell on the hall as everyone listened to Mr Hughes' Spirit-filled and Christ-centred message. At the end of his sermon, Hughes challenged any young people who were prepared to give their lives to Jesus Christ to come down to the front of the hall.

To start with, nobody stirred. Then one lone figure, right from the back of the hall, passed all the other seats and marched to the front. George Thomas was that man. Soon a few more followed, until the front of the hall had one long line of young people.

Recalling this moment, George Thomas later said that he felt as clearly as a man could feel that God was telling him to commit himself to Jesus Christ. George was shy by nature but he knew that it was right for him to overcome his shyness and make a public declaration of the faith he had found that night. And that was why he was the first person on his feet to go down to the front of the hall.

AUGUSTUS MONTAGUE TOPLADY   *Barn*
Hymn-writer   *conversion*

Toplady is best known as the author of the hymn "Rock of ages". He was converted when he listened to a sermon in a barn by James Morris, a Methodist preacher. He says, "Strange that I, who had so long sat under the means of grace in England, should be brought right unto God in an obscure part of Ireland, amidst a handful of people met together in a barn, and by the ministry of one who could hardly spell his own name."

R. A. TORREY   *On the point of suicide*
Evangelist and Bible teacher

On the night of his conversion, when he was 17, Torrey was about to commit suicide. He had been showing off his prowess in the ballroom, but he loathed himself. He smoked, drank to excess, gambled and went with prostitutes and felt trapped in his selfish life. In the middle of the night he searched for his pistol, but in the dark he failed to find it.

At that same moment, his mother was praying for him. He thought of her, and of her faith, and he lifted his heart to God and promised to preach the gospel if God would take his burden.

He kept his promise, studying theology and, with great trepidation, speaking publicly. "It was agony to preach. I was obliged to hold on to something to brace myself up. How happy I used to be every Sunday night. I would say it is over for another week! But one day I learned the lesson that God does not look to me to do the preaching; that it was my privilege to stand up and let him do it. I have had no more dread of the pulpit since then."

ANNE TOWNSEND
After confirmation
Missionary, doctor, writer

The confirmation classes at Anne Townsend's school made Christianity seem totally irrelevant. After the confirmation service itself, nothing seemed to happen and Anne felt disappointed. But a few months later she heard a preacher (at a Youth for Christ rally) explain the concept of sin, and for the first time she understood how Christianity could mean knowing God as a person: Jesus had died to overcome her sin and give her a relationship with God. "It became relevant to me," she said.

DAWSON TROTMAN
Memorizing Bible verses
Founder of the Navigators

Dawson Trotman made what he thought was a decision for Christ on two occasions in his teens, but at the age of 20 he was still unchanged at heart. Arrested while drunk, he remembered his mother telling him she was afraid she would die if she ever heard he was in prison, and he promised God that he would do what God wanted. The policemen let Dawson off with a warning.

He started attending a church, where people were competing to learn Bible verses by heart. He joined in, and learned twenty verses, and found the Holy Spirit brought verses to his mind at specific times to guide his thoughts and actions. He began praying for the eternal life the Bible promised. John 1:12 came to his mind: "Yet to all who received him, to those who believed in his name, he gave the right to become children of God." He prayed to God, not fully comprehending it. "Whatever it means to receive Jesus, I do it right now!"

JAMES USHER
Romans 12:1
17th-century Archbishop of Armagh and student of Bible chronology

At ten years old was the first time that he could remember to have found in himself any evidences of his saving conversion unto God, which was instrumentally wrought by a sermon which he heard preached upon Romans 12:1. "I beseech you brethren by the mercies of God," etc. About the same time also meeting with some notes taken from famous Mr Perkins's works (being not then printed) concerning the sanctification of the Lord's Day, proved, through God's blessing, so effectual with him, that ever after he was the more strict in the observing of it. About the same time also he read over St Augustine's *Meditations*, which so affected him, that he wept often in the reading of them.

A Collection of the Lives of Ten Eminent Divines, Samuel Clarke, Miller, 1662, p. 191

JIM VAUS
"Jim Vaus is dead"
Electronics engineer and former criminal

Jim Vaus felt most ill at ease at a Billy Graham Crusade meeting. He stuck out like a sore thumb. Yet that night his life was radically altered by the decision he made.

It wasn't that Jim was an agnostic or even an atheist. No. Jim believed in God. Jim believed that Jesus Christ was the Son of God and that he was the Saviour of the world.

But on the night of his decision he gave way to the authority of Jesus Christ. This is how he recalls the moment: "I invited Him into my life and, from that time to this, in His strength I've sought to follow Him, to obey Him, and to give Him unhindered access to all of my living. What a change He brought!"

Soon after Vaus had become a Christian and begun to follow Christ, he was offered $10,000 for information to settle a libel case.

Jim told the man, "Haven't you heard? Jim Vaus is dead."

The man thought that Jim had gone mad.

Jim continued, "The person you want to talk to who used to tap wires, make recordings and sell them to the highest bidder, is dead." Then Jim quoted a Bible verse at the man: "If any man be in Christ, he is a new creation" (2 Corinthians 5:17). Jim was determined that everyone should know that he was a new man in Jesus Christ now and that his old life of crime was dead.

HEDLEY VICARS
1 John 1:7
British Army officer killed at Sebastopol

The conversion of Hedley Vicars bears a similarity to that of William Cowper and that of Augustine, in that all three found their minds drawn apparently by chance to a single verse of the Bible.

In November 1851 Captain Vicars was aimlessly turning the pages of a Bible when he came upon this verse from the first letter of John: "The blood of Jesus Christ his Son cleanseth us from all sin" (1 John 1:7). He could not get the words out of his mind; he began to pray, "If this be true for me, henceforth I will live, by the grace of God, as a man should live who has been washed in the blood of Christ."

From that moment on, according to the *Dictionary of National Biography*, "his character was changed. He associated with Dr Twining, the garrison chaplain at Halifax, became a Sunday School teacher, visited the sick, and took every opportunity of reading the scriptures and praying with the men of his company ... Before his regiment left England for the Crimea, early in 1854, it was reported that 'since Mr Vicars became so good, he has steadied about four hundred men in the regiment'."

SAMUEL WALKER
18th-century curate in Truro, Cornwall

All was wrong

Samuel Walker had a reputation for honesty and devotion, yet when the local schoolmaster asked him to convey some "conscience money" to the customs officers the minister was taken aback: the man was, he declared, "verily the first person he had ever met who was truly possessed of the mind of Christ and by whose means he became sensible that all was wrong within and without".

Walker had been attracted to Truro by its social life, but "here God had provided better and quite different things for me, than those which engaged me to come hither. Nothing was further from my thoughts than that I must oppose those very pleasures and engagements of life, the prospect of which led me to Truro. It was in about a year, that principally by the means of a pious Christian friend, whom I found here, I was brought to the knowledge of the ways of God. By and by, I began to deal with the people as lost sinners – my discourses were levelled at self-righteousness and formality, and Christ was preached unto them. From that time God hath done great things for us, and is doing. The number of those who have made particular application to me inquiring what they must do to be saved cannot have been less than eight hundred, of whom, though far the greater part have drawn back, yet I have the pleasure of seeing a very considerable number about me, who, I trust, are sincerely seeking God."

So much had the curate changed that there were some who took exception to him, and asked the rector to dismiss him. The rector tried to do so three times, but recognised the spiritual life in his assistant and finally told the hostile parishioners, "Do you go and dismiss him if you can, I cannot. I feel in his presence as if he were a being of a superior order."

ETHEL WATERS   *"I don't know what to ask"*
Black American Gospel singer

The preacher called to the children to get on their knees and come and pray to the Lord. So Ethel thought she would do it to see what happened. Every night she prayed, though she didn't know what to ask for. Others about her felt cleansed from their sin, or felt close to God; Ethel felt nothing.

Then at the last night of the revival meetings she found peace of heart and peace of mind, and knew she had been searching for that all her life. Her heart was flooded with love and she knew she had found God. For ever afterwards she would have Him as a friend.

Although she could not remember afterwards what she had said or done that night, other people were astonished as they saw her radiance, and she did remember feeling full of light and warmth. She knew that what she had got was not the "wintertime religion" which would wear off by summertime. She knew that she would always know God's protection.

DAVID C. K. WATSON   *A "sophisticated humanist"*
Evangelist and vicar of
St Michael le Belfrey, York

David Watson went to Cambridge University as a "sophisticated humanist". Someone from the Christian Union invited him to a gathering where David was impressed by the gracious manner of the speaker, John Collins. The two met, and David's Old Wellingtonian tie was noticed. Not only did Mr Collins ask if Watson knew Jesus Christ personally – he named three Old Wellingtonians, all of them respected friends of David Watson, who to the same question would not have stammered about being baptized and confirmed, as Watson was doing.

David took home a copy of John Stott's booklet *Becoming a Christian*, read it, asked Jesus into his life and wrote to John Collins telling him what he had done.

As a new Christian, he was nurtured by David Sheppard, then England's cricket captain and later to become bishop of Liverpool; and his encouragement to persist was particularly important since David Watson found his first organized Bible reading "incomprehensible" and his first Christian Union sermon "terrifying"! But on the fifth anniversary of his conversion David was to become John Collins's curate.

H. W. WEBB-PEPLOE   *Conversation by night*
19th-century vicar of St Paul's, Onslow Square, London

His father was a well-to-do parson living in Herefordshire, but Webb-Peploe himself was not converted until shortly before going up to University. Studying with a private tutor and "trying to forget God", he stayed a night with young Henry Wright, a keen Christian. Standing with him on the flat roof of the house under the star-lit sky, Wright spoke to him in a way that made him realise he was a sinner. Wright followed this up next morning by giving him a Bible.

Webb-Peploe drove off to the local races determined to shake away the impression Wright had made on him the previous night. As he arrived at the entrance to the course a young man stopped him, saying, "I beg your pardon sir, would you look at this paper?"

Thinking the young man was illiterate Webb-Peploe began to read the words for him, "Reader, if you died tonight would your soul be in hell?"

Webb-Peploe did not stay for the races. "I turned and

fled, as if God Himself (or Satan) were after me to seize me." Webb-Peploe's conversion was a gradual experience that continued in the following months when he was at Cambridge. A gymnastics accident which laid him on his back with a spine injury a few months later confirmed his faith: "While I was lying on my back expecting to die every week, I got instead of gymnastics the conviction that by the grace of God I knew where I should go to when I died."

SIMONE WEIL
French philosopher
Plainsong and poetry

Simone Weil's first turning towards Christ was when she was visiting Assisi, and felt compelled to pray. The next Easter she spent at a monastery, following the plainsong services and allowing the story of Christ's suffering to enter her being. An English visitor introduced her to George Herbert's poems, one of which she kept reciting until she found she had been praying it and not just saying it. She felt Christ Himself had come down and taken possession of her.

At the time, she was quite ill and was later to die of tuberculosis, but in the midst of her suffering she felt the presence of Christ's love.

She continued to spend many hours in prayer and went to Mass regularly.

JOSEPH AND PAUL WELDON
Evangelists by the printed word
World mission

The Weldon brothers shared a concern to alleviate human suffering worldwide after World War II, and they tried to enlist the help of world religious leaders. They began a lecture tour to spread their idea, but accidents disabled Paul and the tour had to be called off.

Paul started reading the Bible, and discussing it with Joseph; and when they reached the story of Nicodemus in John's Gospel chapter 3 they recognised that here was a religious leader just like so many that they had earlier been corresponding with. They saw how Jesus had died for the redemption of sinners. "We deliberately chose to take God at his word, and were assured that we should see and enter his kingdom in 'due season'."

They wrote to tell their mother about their experience. They wrote to tell the contacts they had all over the world. People started writing back telling them of their own conversions. The correspondence grew, they bought a duplicator, and the work grew to a large and regular printing concern spreading the Word of God all over the world.

CHARLES WESLEY
18th-century Methodist preacher and hymn-writer

The darkness chased away

Charles Wesley's conversion day was 21st May 1738. It was also Pentecost Sunday. He wrote: "I waked in hope and expectation of His coming," but he then experienced "violent opposition and reluctance to believe".

Later, after reading Luther's *Commentary on Galatians*, he wrote: "The Spirit of God strove with my own and the evil spirit, till by degrees He chased away the darkness of my unbelief. I found myself convinced, I knew not how nor when, and immediately fell to intercession. I now found myself at peace with God, and rejoiced in hope of loving Christ. My temper for the rest of the day was mistrust of my own great, but before unknown, weakness. I saw that by faith I stood; by the continual support of faith, which kept me from falling, though of myself I am ever sinking into sin. I went to bed, still sensible of my own weakness, yet confident of Christ's protection."

His brother John, the founder of Methodism, welcomed

the news about his brother's conversion in this way: "I received the surprising news that my brother had found rest to his soul. His bodily strength returned also from that hour."

JOHN WESLEY
18th-century founder of Methodism

"I felt I did trust in Christ"

Before seven in the morning each day Wesley used to pray for two hours and study the Bible for one hour. He then went off visiting prisons and hospitals and teaching people late into the night about the Christian faith.

On his return voyage from America his ship hit a terrific storm. John Wesley had good reason to fear that he would die that night and he was terrified at the thought. Looking at death, Wesley became a frightened man, despite all his Christian teaching and preaching. He asked some fellow travellers who were singing hymns why they were not afraid like him. Their reply was, "If this ship goes down we will go up to be with the Lord for ever." Wesley could not understand where they received such assurance of faith from. All he knew could be summed up in his now famous question, "I came to convert the heathen, but who shall convert me?"

The ship survived the storm and Wesley attended a small chapel in Aldersgate Street in the centre of London. He heard Martin Luther's *Preface to the Book of Romans* being read. It described exactly what John Wesley needed to know at that moment – real faith in Jesus Christ. It spoke about trusting in Jesus Christ for salvation and not trusting in any good works of our own.

John Wesley's Journal entry for that night describes one of the most celebrated Christian conversion stories ever to have taken place. "About a quarter before nine, while he [the preacher at the chapel] was describing the change which God works in the heart through faith in Christ, I felt I did trust in Christ, Christ alone, for salvation, and an assurance was given me that He had taken away my sins, even mine, and saved me from the law of sin and death." May 24, 1738 was the day that John Wesley felt that his heart had been "strangely warmed" by God's grace. After that he travelled over a quarter of a million miles on horseback and on foot preaching this good news about Jesus Christ, as he viewed the whole world as his parish.

PAUL WHITE
Australian doctor, author of the "Jungle Doctor" books
Heart and life

Although he was used to going to church and to Sunday school, Paul White says, "I knew all about the Way, but not how to get on to it." One of the great spiritual influences in his life was his godly mother, who had made him aware of the love of Christ from an early age.

When Paul was 16 years old he attended a meeting held by the fiery Irish evangelist, W. P. Nicholson. Nicholson rather appealed to Paul because he had called their local bishop a "stinking polecat". Paul was surrounded by friends from the church where he was a communicant and a Sunday school teacher. Now he found himself challenged by the agonizing decision of whether to admit in front of them all that he was not really a Christian at all. December 3, 1926 became the day of Paul White's conversion as he decided to go forward to the front of the church as a sign that he had genuinely come to faith in Jesus Christ.

GEORGE WHITEFIELD
18th-century evangelist in Britain and America
A profitable breakfast

The young men called Methodists [because they lived by rule and method] were then much talked of at Oxford. I had heard of, and loved them before I came to the University; and so strenuously defended them when I heard them reviled by the students, that they began to think that I also in time should be one of them.

For above a twelvemonth my soul longed to be acquainted with some of them, and I was strongly pressed to follow their good example, when I saw them go through a ridiculing crowd to receive the Holy Eucharist at St Mary's. At length, God was pleased to open a door. It happened that a poor woman in one of the workhouses had attempted to cut her throat, but was happily prevented. Upon hearing of this, and knowing that both the Mr Wesleys were ready to every good work, I sent a poor apple-woman of our college to inform Mr Charles Wesley of it, charging her not to discover who sent her. She went; but, contrary to my orders, told my name. He having heard of my coming to the castle and a parish-church sacrament, and having met me frequently walking by myself, followed the woman when she was gone away, and sent me an invitation to me by her, to come to breakfast with him the next morning.

I thankfully embraced the opportunity; and, blessed be God! it was one of the most profitable visits I ever made in my life. My soul, at that time, was athirst for some spiritual friends to lift up my hands when they hung down, and to strengthen my feeble knees. He soon discovered it, and like a wise winner of souls, made all his discourses tend that way. And when he had put into my hands Professor Franck's treatise *Against the Fear of Man*, and a book, entitled, *The Country Parson's Advise to his Parishioners* (the last of which was wonderfully blessed to my soul) I took my leave.

In a short time he let me have another book, entitled, *The Life of God in the Soul of Man*; and, though I had fasted, watched and prayed, and received the Sacrament so long, yet I never knew what true religion was, till God sent me that excellent treatise by the hands of my never-to-be-forgotten friend.

Journals, George Whitefield

MARY WHITEHOUSE
Campaigner for media morality

Crossroads

Mary Whitehouse went to Sunday school and enjoyed singing hymns such as "The Day Thou gavest, Lord, is ended".

When she was 24 years old and teaching in Wolverhampton she met up with the Oxford Group and was impressed by these students as a result of attending one of their meetings. Mary realized that she was at a crossroads in her life. She asked these young students from Oxford for their advice and recalls that they replied to her, "If you give your life to God He will guide you and keep you."

Mary followed their advice and gave her life to God, and she has never looked back since. It was the most important turning point in her life.

WILLIAM WILBERFORCE
Parliamentary champion of social reform

Reading and discussion

Wilberforce's home does not appear to have been particularly Christian, though he had an aunt in Wimbledon who had come under the influence of Wesley and Whitefield. The young Wilberforce was staying with her at the time, while attending school. It is not possible to estimate what effect this had on the young lad at that stage because as soon as his mother heard of the aunt's conversion he was taken back home to Hull and sent to the local grammar school. One of the ushers there, however – Isaac Milner – was a deeply religious man who was to have a considerable influence on Wilberforce ...

It was in 1784 that Wilberforce happened to meet Milner again and he invited him to join in a trip to the South of France that he was about to make. On the journey they read and discussed Doddridge's *Rise and Progress of Religion*. This seems to have been the start of a change in Wilberforce's outlook and thinking. There was a further trip with Milner when they read the New Testament in Greek together. A long period of depression followed as Wilberforce became increasingly aware of his own sinfulness, eventually ending up in a visit to see John Newton, vicar of St Mary Woolnoth. This one-time captain of a slave ship, but now on fire for Christ, was able to comfort Wilberforce, and gradually he seems to have arrived at a state of peace and tranquillity as he received the assurance of God's forgiveness. It was not without some apprehension that he shared the subject of his new-found faith with Pitt who, though not himself a believer, still continued to respect and to rely on the advice, support and judgement of his old friend.

Real Christianity, William Wilberforce, edited by Vincent Edmunds,
Hodder & Stoughton, 1989, pp. 7–8

PHILIP WILDING
Writer of westerns and crime fiction
Truth sought

The Wildings began to take an interest in Christianity after their daughter began at Sunday School. Philip felt sure that he had found that truth which he had sought for many years, but it was not until some years later that he publicly committed his life to Christ at an evangelistic meeting.

After his conversion, he continued to have his ups and downs, and learned that though he may accept God's forgiveness, the Christian does not always find it easy to forgive himself.

RON WILLIAMS
Pastor among Australian Aborigines
Acceptance of an outcast

Ron's childhood ambitions were to be a footballer or a boxer or a drunkard, or to go to jail. So poor was the social position of the aboriginal community that drink was all that made them happy and a prison sentence represented the prospect of proper nutrition and even educational opportunity, neither of which they could find outside. An uncle of Ron's had learned to read and write in prison, and brought back good reports of the church services.

Ron's misery was all the greater because the grandfather who had brought him up was killed by hostile tribesmen. Church seemed a chance so Ron went, and was amazed at being welcomed despite his ragged appearance and his unwashed smell. The missionaries even invited him to eat with them – something that no ordinary white person would have done to an Aborigine at the best of times. Ron felt wanted.

Ron was curious to know why these missionaries behaved differently, and when one of them, a white Tasmanian, told how God had changed his life, Ron was ready to ask God to do the same in his own life.

Now he became a changed man: his drinking stopped, he found he could love his stepfather, he went to the new local Bible College and went to work among the men who had killed his grandfather and had been at enmity with his own people for centuries.

MATHILDE WREDE
Finnish prison visitor

John 3:16

The daughter of a provincial governor, Mathilde Wrede lived as a fashionable young lady until she was 19. Then she went to a revivalist meeting and was made to think by the preacher's text – "God so loved the world ..." (John 3:16). She spent that night praying, and from then on she espoused a desire to take the Gospel to prisoners.

One of the first prisoners she visited was a violent man who expected to scare her. She showed no fear of him, and talked to him of the love of God, and so earned his respect that he accepted her New Testament. When he had served his sentence and was released from prison, he was a committed Christian who went out to make reparation to his victims.

JACK WYRTZEN
Evangelist and founder of the American "Word of Life" radio programmes

Jack Wyrtzen greatly admired the courage of his friend George Schilling who had recently changed from being the heaviest drinker among the New York National Guard to kneeling next to his bed each night to read his Bible and pray. However, Jack joined in the general teasing and shoe-throwing against George Schilling. Jack tore up the copies of John's Gospel that George kept on giving him until he eventually sat down and read one of them.

The turning point in Jack's life came when George invited him to play a trombone solo for a Gospel meeting that was to be held in Brooklyn. Jack agreed to go because he was curious and for the sake of his friend George. He learned the hymn, played it and then sat back to listen to the rest the meeting.

When the preacher started to use lots of religious jargon like "new birth" and "putting your trust in Jesus Christ" and "having a personal Saviour" Jack was irritated. By the time the preacher moved into top gear and shouted out his message about a lake of fire in hell and God's coming judgement, Jack was angry that any preacher should try and frighten people in this way.

Jack left the meeting a disturbed man because he thought that if hell existed then perhaps heaven might exist as well. Alone in his bedroom in the middle of the night, he found himself feeling afraid because of his own pride. He wondered if what he had read about Jesus Christ in John's Gospel might be true. Then the Holy Spirit stepped in and convicted Jack of his sin and convinced him that Jesus did indeed die for him. Jack got out of bed and knelt down and committed his life to Jesus Christ.

GEORGE YOSHIMI
Converted Buddhist

Born to a Japanese family who had settled in the United States, Yoshimi was a Buddhist but sensed an unrest he could not easily pinpoint. Because he had a sister who was a Christian, he began to learn about Christian doctrine, but although he was impressed he still believed the Buddha could get him to heaven.

Eventually, after having been pulled this way and that by conflicting loyalties, he listened to a committed Christian explaining about salvation, and decided to commit his life to Christ. "From that day on," he wrote, "my life has never been the same. It was the most important decision I have ever made. All my burdens were lifted and I was a new man."

ZACCHAEUS
1st-century tax collector in Jericho

Jesus entered Jericho and was passing through. A man was there by the name of Zacchaeus; he was a chief tax collector and was wealthy. He wanted to see who Jesus was, but being a short man he could not, because of the crowd. So he ran ahead and climbed a sycamore-fig tree to see him, since Jesus was coming that way.

When Jesus reached the spot, he looked up and said to him, "Zacchaeus, come down immediately. I must stay at your house today." So he came down at once and welcomed him gladly.

All the people saw this and began to mutter, "He has gone to be the guest of a 'sinner'."

But Zacchaeus stood up and said to the Lord, "Look, Lord! Here and now I give half of my possessions to the poor, and if I have cheated anybody out of anything, I will pay back four times the amount."

Jesus said to him, "Today salvation has come to this house,

because this man, too, is a son of Abraham. For the Son of Man came to seek and to save what was lost."

Luke 19:1–10